Thomas Neunert

Strategic Management and U.S. Health Care

MARQUETTE
GENERAL HEALTH SYSTEM

A Case Study

Thomas Neunert

Strategic Management and U.S. Health Care

Marquette General Health System

A Case Study

ibidem-Verlag
Stuttgart

Die Deutsche Bibliothek - CIP-Einheitsaufnahme:

Ein Titeldatensatz für diese Publikation ist bei
Der Deutschen Bibliothek erhältlich

∞

Gedruckt auf alterungsbeständigem, säurefreien Papier
Printed on acid-free paper

ISBN: 3-89821-187-8

Printed in Germany

It is perfectly true, as philosophers say,
That life must be understood backwards.
But they forget the other proposition
That it must be lived forwards.

Søren Kierkegaard, 1843

Content Overview

Contents

Illustrations and Tables

Abbreviations

AAMC	Association of Medical Colleges
ACS	American College of Surgeons
AIDS	Acquired Immuno-Deficiency Syndrome
AHA	American Hospital Association
AMA	American Medical Association
BBA	Balanced Budget Act
CAH(N)	Critical Access Hospital (Network)
CEO	Chief Executive Officer
CFO	Chief Finance Officer
CON	Certificate of Need
CT	Computer Topography
DRG	Diagnosis Related Group
DSH	Disproportional Share Hospital
EKG	Electro-Cardiogram
FRG	Federal Republic of Germany
FTC	Federal Trade Commission
GDP	Gross Domestic Product
GDR	German Democratic Republic
HCFA	Health Care Financing Administration
HMO	Health Maintenance Organization
HR	Human Resources
IME	Indirect Medical Education
Inc.	Incorporated
IT	Information Technology
JCAHO	Joint Commission on Accreditation of Healthcare Organizations
LLC	Limited Liability Corporation
MD	Medical Doctor
MGH	Marquette General Hospital
MGHS	Marquette General Health System
MHA	Michigan Health and Hospital Association
MRI	Magnetic Resonance Imaging

OB	Organizational Behavior
PAC	Political Action Committee
PT	Physical Therapy
OP	Occupational Therapy
RHCIA	Rural Health Care Improvement Act
SSA	Social Security Agency
SWOT(s)	Strengths, Weaknesses, Opportunities, Threats
U.P.	Upper Peninsula
UPHP	U.P. Health Plan
UPHCN	Upper Peninsula Health Care Network
U.S. (US-)	United States

Foreword

This book is my thesis in Political Science, the final work of my Master's studies at the University of Hanover, Northern Germany. The research subject and the method-choice of a case study had its starting point in an internship in marketing and community relations at Marquette General Health System in 1999. Meeting with community leaders, politicians and customers and observing market research activities of the department as well as the strategic planning process of MGHS, I became interested in further academic research. Having to write a Master's thesis to earn the German 'Magister Artium' as a student of Political Science and Social Psychology, these internship observations and the perception of MGHS became a possible object for this thesis in one of my main subjects – public policy and health care administration.
These plans materialized and resulted in this thesis about U.S. Health Care and Strategic Management at MGHS. Besides its technical foundation, this thesis and the way it was institutionally set between the USA and Germany had another basis: The support, the encouragement and advice of many people in terms of providing a stimulating educational background for the ideas developed and the perspectives taken in this thesis.

I would especially like to thank Dr. Ileana and Dr. John W. Renfrew who hosted me during my research stays in Marquette, Robert J. Raica, Assistant Administrator, John R. Howko, Director of Education, and others at MGHS who promoted my intentions researching in the hospital as well as Jim Lajoie, Jens Knye and Dirk Ahlers who shared their expertise in academic writing, data processing and "American life issues" with me.

This book is dedicated to my parents Waltraud and Hans. Thanks for your love, concern and support!

1 Study Design and Methods

1.1 Theme, Object and Research

The theme of this study corresponds with the insight I received during my internship at MGHS. The subject 'U.S. Health Care and Strategic Management' covers my areas of interest and reflects best the socio-political situation surrounding Marquette General Health System. The strategic planning process of MGHS was interesting for me, because of the diverse legislative, socio-economic and ethical demands the hospital, being a non-profit rural health care provider, had to cope with.
Observing this strategic management process from a European perspective, made it necessary for me to first scan the principles and the setting of American and U.S. health care delivery.
The object of research was the 'Strategic Management' of Marquette General Health System (MGHS), a non-profit health care provider in the Upper Peninsula (U.P.) of Michigan in the USA between 1995 and 1999. The non-profit status represents the interesting cut between a market-based and social-responsible behavior of, for example, communities granting tax-exemption for receiving the provision of uncompensated care for the community.
'Marquette General Health System (MGHS),' the official name since 1998, is representing the whole health system including diverse facilities besides the main base on the Upper Peninsula. In the past, it was named Marquette General Hospital (MGH). This object and its rural setting provide a good laboratory situation. Factors influencing MGH(S) are lucid and practical to survey in difference to a dense health care environment found in larger metropolitan areas.

The research question had to narrow the broad range of issues between U.S. health care and strategic management. This study is to reveal how a health care provider in a market based system strategically prepares itself for diverse outside and inside influences on its business, no matter if they are of a social, economic or political nature. My German background and socialized medicine as basic concept in Middle Europe determines the perspective of the questions that arose: In what way does a U.S. health care provider follow market and ethic demands? Does non-profit ensure quality health care? How does this ethic mission work out, if the surrounding system is mainly market based? And do we find action plans, that are worth being transferred to the German system, and if so, why? Those were the questions to which I wanted to obtain deeper answers. My overall scientific guiding question for all this reads as follows:

What does strategic planning of a U.S. non-profit health care provider look like in the tense relationship of ethic mission, and economic margin?

1.2 Study Design

The use of a case study research as methodological vehicle developed through the kind of questions I had in mind. That were questions like 'how...?', and 'what kind of...?' to explore and determine the strategic management process of MGHS.

Thus the study's character is a composition of a descriptive and explanatory study. A theoretic framework had to be developed. Propositions were stated to define the direction of research that were based on the set of initial questions.

These propositions also enabled me to formulate a conclusion by applying the case study related measure of 'pattern-matching'. In the final step of this work the findings had to be evaluated and I had to determine if and with which pattern (propositions) the results match. The question was if the strategy chosen at MGHS as for 1995 to 1999 matched the demands of the mission or the economic interests and how this can be generalized with regard to Germany.

That is the overall study design. As for the internal structure, it was appropriate to choose a multiple-unit design for this case study. Compared with a single-unit (holistic) design this had the advantage to cover a broader range of issues like the various business areas of MGH(S) as well as economical, historical and social aspects.

1.3 Research Propositions

These propositions guided the research to find answer to the author's questions.

1.) Marquette General's main goal as a non-profit provider is to focus primarily on the ethical mission and, secondly on the economic margin. This shows in their business activity: community relations before asset management e.g.

2.) The U.S. market economy and the individualized mentality of the society make social-responsible health care provision impossible.

3.) Between the upper and lower management level clear differences about what the overall business policy and strategy should be like, are supposed to exist. The upper management is supposed to follow rational principles to keep the system running economically. The lower management being closer to the patient's needs, thinks about what is best for the help-seeking individual.

4.) For German hospital providers facing a tendency toward increased market forces changing the face of hospital management, U.S. general hospitals and the American way to do business in the tense relationship between ethical and economic demands are particularly interesting to learn from.

The mentioned propositions are believed to be true in the circumstances regarding the study's object and boundaries that set the limits for research.

1.4 Boundaries

This research is limited:

- Scientifically: To data related to the general context regarding the population for customers of MGHS. This social context is not especially diversified into ethnicity for example – this might be useful in a sociological approach.
- Locally: To the area where MGHS operates, that is Marquette County and the Upper Peninsula of Michigan. Regarding the observation of legislation and politics the focus area is extended to Michigan, the USA and Germany.
- Institutionally: To a U.S. American non-profit health care provider, the general hospital MGH/MGHS. MGHS, when observing topics regarding the entire health system and MGH, when looking at the Marquette based main facility.

- With regard to time: That is primarily strategic management between 1995 and 1999. Only the facts about the history of the US-health system and facts that are needed to explain the environment of this process extend these boundaries.

1.5 Units of Research

The purpose of the following five units is to gather a data basis highlighting the institutional setting of MGHS and to clarify the way of U.S. health care.

- 'History of U.S. Health Care' to explore the basic roots;
- 'Health Care Economics' to collect information: What is significant for market-based health care and on which theories is it grounded;
- 'Health Care Legislation within the Late 1990s' to observe hospital related federal and state legislation;
- 'The Institutional Setting of MGHS' with the sub units 'The Institutional History' and 'The (Geographical) Location' to characterize the object.
- 'Organizational Theory and The Strategic Plan of 1996' provided the frame to investigate the strategic planning process of MGHS.

The sixth unit focuses on 'Strategic Thinking and Concrete Actions' on the administrative level in form of three categories and further sub units:

A) The perspective of the 'Chief Executive Officer (CEO) and General Administration', the 'Chief Finance Officer (CFO) and 'Finance and Business Development', the 'Board of Trustees and Governing Non-Profit MGHS'

B) The administrative perspective in human resources; nursing and home health; community relations and marketing; program and network management.

C) A further breakdown of the community relations and marketing department into 'Pastoral Care, Patient Relations, Physician Recruitment/Relation.' The purpose of finally breaking down overall strategic planning additionally to the mentioned selected areas is to explore areas that have a broad overview onto proceedings and activities at MGHS besides the main ones.

1.6 Data Collection

The scientific methods the data collection is based on are in particular:

- Collection of written documents (strategic plans, customer reports, surveys, brochures, web-pages and secondary literature)
- Evaluation of personal observations stored as memos of planning actions within and regarding MGHS during the internship and during a three-months stay at Marquette in winter 1999/2000.
- Evaluation of personally conducted interviews with the CEO, the Secretary of the Board of Trustees, the CFO, the Assistant Administrators and two selected department heads regarding specialty of pastoral care and patient relation in the States. These interviews were open interviews. First, a concept of strategic management was formulated based on the knowledge received from priorly collected data, like written documents or observatory memos. Secondly, variables were assigned to this concept, reflecting the several management areas' approaches in order to find out in which composition these variables built up MGHS's concept of overall strategic management. The last step was to formulate questions that represent these variables.
- Personal conduction of anonymous questionnaires sent out to all 121 MGHS department heads and program directors. 44 of those, which is 36.4 percent, were sent back and were evaluated. These questionnaires were to control if the lower management had the same or a differing view onto strategic management. Therefore, the same concept and variables were taken as in the interviews with the administrators, the CFO and the CEO and the Board level, to make the results of the interviews comparable with those of the questionnaires. The department heads were asked to rate certain propositions as right, true or agreeable on a five-point-scale from 'not at all,' over 'not very much,' 'don't know,' 'much' to 'very much.'

1.7 Analysis of Data

In order to check which propositions to determine prior to the object of study or how to rate them if propositions finally matched with the reality, the collected data had to be analyzed and interpreted.

1.7.1 Qualitative Content Analysis

This method was applied to documents, memos and the interview material. This qualitative analysis of the material's content included interpretation through primary summarizing and secondary hermeneutic interpretation. The basic way and goal of interpretation of an analysis is to characterize something. Therefore, the collected data minimized by assigning so-called code units and context units within the entire material, for example, words or phrases. These will be further interpreted in the next step. The units have to be categorized by transforming their content into paraphrases. Each unit forming a new category has to

a) be congruent with the research topic and
b) highlight a new aspect within the context units

All trivial data or data that do not match with the context unit, are excluded from the final amount of material. If no additional new categories can be found, the remaining data units are assigned to those categories depending on the level of abstraction chosen through paraphrasing. In a last step the paraphrases within their categories can be generalized and taken for further exclusion or condensation of data. This method of summarizing is to reduce the material in a way that the main features of the material are kept, but a new and easier comprehensible material basis can be received still representing the entire material.

1.7.2 Hermeneutic Circling

The summarized data or the received paraphrases need (as described above) further interpretation to get beyond a formal summary of the data. Hermeneutic interpretation means comparing the material in a dialectic two-way-direction with one's own opinion – this is also called 'hermeneutic circling' between data and own opinion. This procedure resulting in the formulation of conclusion is done on a matrix of the already existing knowledge about the material's and the interpreter's background. The (opinion-related) conclusions should not formulated as facts, but as new hypotheses, that are subject for further approval. When reading the last chapters of this thesis, my conclusion has to be understood in that way.

1.7.3 Quantitative Data Analysis

In this survey the data was ranked on a nominal scale. Here ratios between certain variables cannot be determined. The rating 'very much' is not two times better than 'much.' We cannot assign numbers as '2' for 'very much' and '1' for 'much.' If 10 persons rate one item as 'very much important' and 20 persons rate another item as 'important,' we cannot conclude that both items actually have the same importance within the entire focus group. Therefore, only the ratings only for each item are added and these amounts are then interpreted in the sense of being important, decisive or indecisive, unimportant.

1.8 Line of Discussion

The line of discussion goes from the history of U.S. health care over to the institutional and sociological setting of MGHS within the Upper Peninsula of Michigan over to the strategic planning process and business strategy of this hospital system to the application onto the diverse departments and services represented by the main administrative areas, like finance or human resources.

A specially deep insight is taken in the last area dealing with a broad range of strategy-related factors: The area of community relations and marketing represents nearly all areas the hospital is involved. That is why the report of action plans is then broken down further to the three main customer service areas within community relations: patient relations, pastoral care and physician recruitment.

After summarizing the results with regard to the research question my own view comes into play within a conclusion about strategic management by MGHS between 1995 and 1999 and the stated propositions. This view will be rounded off, taking a look onto potential learning aspects that can be transformed into the German health care environment.

2 History of Health Care in the United States

2.1 The Beginnings of Medical Service in America

The process of immigration and the colonization of America brought people from an already coined cultural background into a country where the immigrants had to build a completely new system of social service developing over time. Physicians in colonial America differed very much from the modern primary care provider or specialist. They were not trained or licensed as it is common today. No medical school existed at that time. Basic medical service was provided by a few physicians, trained in Europe and by some apothecaries. Only one hospital existed for a few years in Philadelphia. At the end of the American Revolutionary War, about 3500 established practitioners were serving in colonial America and more than 400 of these had received some formal training. The first medical school, established in 1756 at the College of Pennsylvania, released a very little number of licensed physicians in the sense of professional standardized training, mostly in form of apprenticeships. Since 1773, aspiring physicians paid a fee for education, receiving a certificate upon completion of the five-year curriculum. This certified training was a basic step towards a structured health care system.

Since the late 1800s, care provision by medical practitioners or physicians developed in the newly founded United States of America through broadened and standardized medical education. The foundation of medical schools, for example at the University of Pennsylvania, offering a kind of systematic organization of apprenticeships was a meaningful step to setting up standards for the health profession and improving the level of care.

Medical practitioners were certified on a local basis by the hospital, where students have only apprenticed, the graduation of university, or a combination of both. Up to the time of a licensing mechanism as quality standard for health care, which was first started at the University of Georgia in 1821, the physicians' competence was measured by the standard of whether or not the physician had graduated from a medical school with medical degree. The early hospitals in the United States can be seen as instruments in the 1800s, fighting back the growing number of diagnosed diseases through progress in science. However, primarily most of them were shelters for the aged and infirm, orphans, vagrants, and the maimed; a protection for the inhabitants of a community from communicable diseases; and as an emergency quarter to accommodate wounded soldiers, e.g. during wartime. The image of these early hospitals was rather bad within the population. Hospitals were seen as crowded and unsanitary, where the danger for the own health was usually greater than at home. Over time, this situation changed through medical progress and the expansion of public health through charitable intentions of religious organizations.

Between the beginning of the seventeenth century and the Revolutionary War, health care delivery cannot be separated from the general socio-political situation of America as a destination for immigration.

In Europe, political turmoil and poor living circumstances made people leave their home country. America became attractive for immigrants. Missionaries – Jesuits, Franciscans and Dominicans – followed to implement religious values in the new world, first mainly in New France. In 1639, nuns from France established a first emergency hospital in Quebec to treat victims of epidemics, like typhus, smallpox and yellow fever, native American massacres, poverty and war.

In the English colony of north America, the initial approach to social service was different. Not the Catholic church, as it was the case with the French or Spanish parts through missionaries, did first stamp the system. Here, Emigrants - independent middle-class people from agricultural, mercantile and artisan groups - were mostly dissenters from the Church of England. If anyone provided health service to these materially poor, then this was managed by individuals often untrained in health care. Saldom, hospitals in the English dominated areas were existing within the 1600s. More common were occasionally shelters for sick people disembarking from the emigrant ships.

Focusing on the English colony and later USA, the number of hospitals in the English colony after 1700 rose steadily and became more diversified. In many communities, smaller private hospitals were set up by their physician or surgeon owners for people recovering from the effect of inoculation, for surgical cases, or for maternity patients. Three categories point out the hospital sector of that time:

Almshouses: The almshouses of the 1800s and their hospital departments provided care mostly for poor patients or their families.

Voluntary Hospitals: Since the 1850s, these new institutions offered health care to people who were able to pay and voluntarily seeked institutional help, for example, at the Pennsylvania Hospital, the New York Hospital or the Massachusetts General Hospital. The foundation of the latter was a private initiative of two physicians convincing influential citizens to establish a charitable hospital.

Church Hospital: Like so often in the past, the Catholic church played a meaningful role in the spreading of hospital foundations. One example is the De Paul Hospital in St. Louis incepted in 1828. These church hospitals were sponsored through gifts of wealthy church affiliated citizens and ensured ongoing medical service.[1]

These non-governmental health care approaches do not mean that there was no initiative of the Federal Government to take care of the people's health. However, they were practiced only in a rudimentary or subsidiary way. For the time being, the role of the federal government was to protect the society from the common risks, such as epidemic disease, and to meet the essential needs of the poor and destitute coupled with support of religious and other charitable agencies, like fraternal societies, lodges and immigrant clubs. The year 1798 then marked the beginning of systematically based health care within the United States through the first federal health legislation: The Marine Hospital Service Act provided medical care for sick and disabled seamen. This service was financed through a taxation of seaman. This financing of service influenced the health service expansion in general. Public Health - first mostly quarantine - set standards and highlighted the need for widespread health care.[2]

2.2 Hospitals in the 1800s

Between 1840 and 1900 the number of hospitals rose more than before. The government took an active interest in public health care, recognizing the additional need through epidemics like the yellow fever around the Civil War. This increased demand and governmental public health action is one reason for the hospital boom, the advanced science and the foundation of many non-governmental hospitals like church hospitals over this period. The later period of the time, the more diverse are the categories of hospitals. The focus of this study, however, will mainly be on General Hospitals.

2.2.1 General Hospitals

At the times of Thomas Jefferson, only the mentioned two predecessors of general hospitals (in Philadelphia and New York) existed and the majority of inpatients beds was provided in almshouses.[3] "The hospital was a characteristic product of the society that nurtured it. The hospital could not help but reproduce fundamental social relationships and values in microcosm. Early America was a society in which relationships of class and status described public demeanors and specified the particular responsibilities of individuals and the community. Allied with medicine's limited technical resources, it produced a medical system minimally dependent on institutional care, in which dependence and social status, not diagnosis, determined the makeup of institutional populations. Without [certification by a hospital contributor and] such personal knowledge ... a prospective patient should occupy an almshouse pallet and not a private hospital bed."[4]

This limited institutional care changed through ongoing social, economic, and scientific progress after 1840: Growing "economic and political independence ... [and] the principles of American democracy engendering the spirit of equality, the spread of popular education [and an increasing number of immigrants from Europe resulting in] vigorous intellectual activity ... were paramount factors in the expansion of hospitals [because of] the advantages in nursing and the medical sciences."[5]

A hospital applying these demanded socio-political standards was the John Hopkins Hospital in Baltimore. John Hopkins, a multimillionaire, sponsored the erection of this hospital and a university in 1867. The condition he made that most of the patients should be "indigent sick of the city admitted without charge, without regard to age, sex or color ... a limited number of patients might also be admitted who were able to pay for their care was outstanding and new. Though the influence of religion should be present, the administration should not yield to any sectarian discipline or control."[6] A democratic community hospital was born.

Another factor, which is one of the most decisive factors for the foundations of hospitals for the general public, was the already mentioned Civil War. The army hospitals provided diverse models for new scientific and systematic treatment methods for later civilian hospitals. Especially the Civil War brought to light the glaring deficiencies of in broad medical treatment and nursing.

Advanced medical science had a further impact on a strengthened systematic health care. Hospitals were the first that implemented new standards or simply enabled new technical methods, for example, in surgery or the first use of anesthesia at Massachusetts General Hospital 1846.[7]

2.3 The 1900s Changing the Face of Health Care

In this century, the face of primarily health care delivery depending on private force not only changed through completing governmental actions but also through development of insurance to cover the people's health care needs. The government's legislation shows what health care for the public was planned to be. After the Marine Health Service Act, the enactment of the Social Security Act in 1935 marked the definite end of considering health only a personal matter. The basic concepts were:

1.) "Social insurance for the working population, that is, unemployment insurance, workers compensation, and guaranteed retirement benefits [and]
2.) Public assistance, that is, direct financial aid provided by the states for those unable to work. Although not intended as a medical insurance program, this

precedent-setting law provided federal grants for public health, maternal and child health."[8]

To pay for social services was a critical change for the mainly pure market basis of health care that developed over the last centuries.

A next step in the development of broad health care was the medical care program for farmers set up by the Farm Security Administration from 1935 to 1947. This legislation is an important prototype of governmental bottom-up strategy on health care delivery by particular programs. This first federal program included consumer participation, decentralization of care, centralization of payment source, prevention and health education, the use of nurse clinicians, salaried physicians, and controls on referrals and hospitalization.

The Hill-Burton Construction Act of 1946 was a federal provider promoting initiative, directly benefitting hospitals. It gave monetary assistance to hospitals that had economically suffered under the depression before World War II. The influence of the federal administration increased in 1965-66 again with the passage of legislation providing money for the establishment of regional medical programs, comprehensive health planning, extensive aid to medical professional education and amendments to the Social Security Act of 1965 – Medicare and Medicaid.[9]

Similar to the effect of the Social Security amendments and the planned financing of Hospital erections through the Hill-Burton Construction Act was the effect of the parallel development of a private net of insurance and prepaid plans, such as Blue Cross/Blue Shield in the 1930s. All this should ensure health care also for those people, who were not wealthy enough or willing to pay health care expenditure directly out of pocket.

These initiatives of the Federal Government and the States to direct and control further health care delivery for a broader part of the population is a completion of private insurance plans. Charitable care as cultural diversity through immigration can be seen as a decisive characterization for the bottom-up, market-based system.

In the late nineteenth century, already Germany under Chancellor Bismarck chose a different way by implementing a governmental-driven, top-down Welfare-system with a broad coverage in a very early time of the industrial time epoch.

So much about the evolution of the American health care delivery. Further on, the other side has to be highlighted: costs and their genesis, access to care and payment-coverage. This has to be done before the main evolutionary issues are summarized.
In the beginning of health care in America and in the United States the churches played a critical role. Health care was further provided through individual services. Such private health care providers worked independently nearly without any interaction. Immigration strengthened this individual approach. A change came with the erection of the first large hospitals, the beginning of organized care delivery.
After World War II, the major changes in social and political life as well as the technical aspects of the industrial revolution made grow the interest in the social and organizational structure of health care. This process was promoted through the newly developed payment plans and insurance, first through private companies, then additionally through federal legislation like Medicare and Medicaid. Health Care became a public issue not only one for wealthy people.[10] The government's role was:

- Assuring availability of care to all; contributory financed Medicare or/and via general tax revenue financed Medicaid.
- Extension of publicly financed services
- Setting standards to ensure the quality of medical services
- Provision of services through non-government providers wherever possible
- Financial support for modernization, construction and equipment of health care facilities and education of the respective personnel.

This approach to the goal of subsidiary support follows a bottom-up strategy, where the private force comes first and the government's coverage is rather a last resort. It is a model of essential pragmatic health care legislation having the intention to return people to the workforce and investing into the future. Thus American Health Care has its roots in market-based health care and financial coverage, despite the strong Catholic impact of e.g. the reliance in the Protestant ethic.[11]

2.4 Medical Expenditures and Coverage within the History

2.4.1 Self-payment and Philanthropy

Until the advent of Medicare and Medicaid, philanthropic gifts were a major source of funds for medical care. Traditionally, hospital trustees were expected to contribute substantially to the financing of their hospitals. It was expected from physicians to offer services for the poor without charging them. In return hospitals were sometimes letting physicians use room and equipment to treat their 'paying' patients. After coverage of many services through governmental programs, philanthropy helped to sponsor education, research, demonstration programs, etc.[12]

2.4.2 Private Insurance

The first private insurance was the individual accident insurance in 1850. Since 1910, one company provided a kind of group health insurance for a firm's employees. Since World War II, wages were frozen. So, additional offerings of insurance plans played a decisive role in collective bargaining to attract employees beside the essential wage. The expression 'Private insurance companies' covers two types: Insurance companies and prepaid group insurance plans like 'Blue Cross/Blue Shield.'

2.4.3 Prepaid Group Insurance

By 1937, the medical societies of California, Michigan and Pennsylvania were sponsoring physician service plans. The large spreading in nearly every state and their later ownership (until 1972) by the American Medical Association (AMA) reflects the need of medical providers to improve the ability of patients to pay for service. The basic principles formulated in 1938 of Blue Cross/Blue Shield are:

- They are non-profit organizations and hold low cash reserves,
- The board of directors has to represent hospitals, physicians, and the public,
- The board of directors has to be supervised by state insurance departments,
- Employees are on salary and agents are not paid on commission,
- They emphasize 'service' as hospital benefits rather than 'cash indemnities',
- They are geographically separated and should not compete with each other.

These prepaid health plans are limited to a single or a group of States contracting with service providers. Service benefits are given to insured persons. Payments are made directly to doctors (through Blue Shield) and hospitals (through Blue Cross) ruled by special enabling legislation.[13] They differ from private insurance: They don't have the goal to make profit by filling the gap of needed risk coverage within the population.

2.4.4 Health Maintenance Organizations (HMO)

In difference to special risk covering insurance, HMOs deliver comprehensive health care for a set monthly fee for from the enrollees. Applying the method of prepayment means predicting and planning economical outcomes. HMO's have their roots in the year 1721. The largest HMO, Kaiser Permanente Health Plan, is determined as follows:

- Private nonprofit organization, financing and provision of care are combined
- Fixed premium payment (prepayment): Community-rated fixed monthly dues paid primarily through the members' employer
- Medical Groups Practice with physicians paid on a capitation, rather than a fee-for-service basis, capitation payments are made to hospitals through Kaiser and physicians through Permanente on a fixed monthly basis regardless of use
- Hospital based: The group practice is physically combined with an owned hospital
- Voluntary enrollment: People are not automatically enrolled by the employer
- Comprehensiveness: Wide range of benefits without deductibles or coinsurance[14]

This diversity of private insurance systems was based on the fact that coverage of health care expenditures were not guided by an overall government-offered health plan as it is in the case of Germany. This changed with two governmental programs.

2.4.5 Medicare and Medicaid

Under Medicare, health care for Americans over 65 and the disabled was provided. This program was administered by the Social Security Agency (SSA) and the Health Care Financing Administration (HCFA) on a federal level. A rate of 53.8 percent of the federal funding was spent for Medicare covered expenditures, 27.1 percent for Medicaid, a state administered program under oversight of the HCFA covered a share of about 39 percent of local and state based health care expenditures for the poor.
This 1965 enactment represented the bottom-line to provide coverage of health expenditures only for needy groups vs. a model that stands for universal coverage provided by the federal government on a compulsory basis financed by taxes or earnings. Similar federal programs for maternal and infant care followed through President Johnson's War on Poverty during the 1960s.[15] The later de-

velopments of the health system in the second half of the 1900s and 'new' problems like rising expenditures are object of the next chapter.

---

[1] See Raffel, M. W. (1980). *The U.S. Health System – Origins and Functions.* Page 2-7 and 202-222.

[2] See Litman, T. J. and Robins, L. S. (1997). *Health Politics and Policy.* Page 445.

[3] Long, D. E. and Golden, J. (1989). *The American General Hospital.* Page 4.

[4] Long, D. E. and Golden, J. (1989). *The American General Hospital.* Page 5.

[5] Raffel, M. W. (1980) *The U.S. Health System – Origins and Functions.* Page 227 and see page 226.

[6] Raffel, M. W. (1980). *The U.S. Health System – Origins and Functions.* Page 244.

[7] Raffel, M. W. (1980). *The U.S. Health System – Origins and Functions.* Page 233-242.

[8] Litman, T. J. and Robins, L. S. (1997). *Health Politics and Policy.* Page 23.

[9] Litman, T. J. and Robins, L. S. (1997). *Health Politics and Policy.* Page 23.

[10] See Lancaster, Jeanette. (1999). *Nursing Issues in Leading and Managing Change.* Page 7-9.

[11] See Litman, T. J. and Robins, L. S. (1997). *Health Politics and Policy.* Page 23-25.

[12] Wilson, F. A. and Neuhauser, D. (1982). *Health Services in the United States.* Page 119 and see page 119-120.

[13] Wilson, F. A. and Neuhauser, D. (1982) *Health Services in the United States.* Page 109 and see page 110.

[14] Wilson, F. A. and Neuhauser, D. (1982) *Health Services in the United States.* Page 112-114.

[15] Patel, K. and Rushefsky, M. E. (1995). *Health Care Politics and Policy in America.* Page 15-16, 36 and 51 pp.

3 Approaches to Health Care 1960-2000

3.1 Health Expenditures and Socioeconomic Facts

This chapter deals with the later history of health care delivery in the United States. Market forces were promoting the development with much private initiative and only little governmental control up to World War II. In the younger history, rising costs and expenditures made the need for cost containment attempts develop. Regulatory approaches to deliver health care in a efficient way were taken by the government to answer this problem which can be outlined as follows:

- The sum of national health care expenditures has steadily grown
- Since the implementation of Medicare and Medicaid, especially governmental federal and state expenditures for health rose, too
- Health expenditures spent through hospital services increased, too.[1]

The HCFA tables in the appendix provide the complete overview over the development of healthcare expenditures, which are the sum of all health services and supplies (expenditures for personal health care, program administration, net costs of private health insurance, and public health) and research and construction. What other factors apart from the increase in health care expenditures can be found?

Health expenditures increased steadily over the decades. However, this increase slowed down after 1990, and in 1998 the expenditures rose faster again. Since the enactment of the Social Security Programs Medicare and Medicaid, the amount of health expenditures rose from \$26.9 billion in 1960 to \$1228.5 billion in 1999, also the Gross Domestic Product (GDP) rose. The numbers for health expenditures as a percent of the GDP give a more meaningful insight stating how much the area of health industry grew in relation to the whole economy: While health expenditures were 5.1 percent of the GDP in 1960, this percentage

rose to 13.9 percent in 1999 being stable or only slightly fluctuating around 13.7 percent since the early nineties. That means, the health care sector expanded and is expanding more than other U.S. business sectors.[2]
The most booming areas were the hospital care sector, with a steady increase from $9.3 billion in 1960 to $382.8 billion in 1998. However, that was not the only growing field within personal health care. Corresponding with the disproportional growing share of older U.S. residents - being one decisive but not the only reason - also the nursing home care and home health area showed large increases over the recent decades and years. The nursing home care sector's expenditures grew from $0.8 billion in 1960 to $87.8 billion in 1998 and the home health care sector's expenditures from $0.1 billion in 1960 to 29.3 billion in 1998. The area of physician services has to be mentioned as one with large increase rates. While in 1960, $5.3 billion were spent in this field of personal health care, 1998 $229.5 billion were spent for physician services.[3]

The third interesting aspect is to point out the development of health care funding in the States over the years by percent and source: Generally, there is a bias between public and private funding with a strong preponderance of private funding. This shows the importance of the private role versus the governmental role in the general political and sociological setting of the United States. Nevertheless, the share of public funding of health care expenditures rose from 24.8 percent in 1960 to 46.2 percent in 1997 and decreased again to 45.5 percent in 1998. Private funding accordingly decreased from 75.2 percent in 1960 relatively steady to 53.8 percent in 1997 and increased to 54,5 percent in 1998. Especially the federal administration came more into play over the decades. Federal funding increased (see Medicare/Medicaid) from 10.9 percent in 1960 to 33.4 percent in 1997 and decreased to 32.8 percent in 1998. However, the share of state and local funding stayed on a relative stable level of 13.9 percent in 1960 and 12.7 percent in 1998.[4]

Looking at the respective shares of payments for personal health care expenditures, the following were the largest growing over the last decades. In 1960, privately out-of-pocket payments were with 55.3 percent the largest source besides private insurance with a 21.2 percent-share and state or local payments with 12.6 percent. Third-party-payers totally covered 44.7 percent. This changed after the implementation of Medicare and Medicaid at the mid of the sixties and over the 1970s and 1980s: In 1998 all third-party-payers covered 80.4 percent of the personal health expenditures. Private insurance plans covered 28.6 percent in 1980 and 33.1 percent in 1998. The government paid through federal, state or local programs 40.1 percent in 1980 and 43.6 percent in 1998, in which federal covered the bigger part. After 1997, all third-party-payment shares decreased slightly. Only the share of private out-of-pocket payments increased. [5]

3.2 Theory of Health Care Economy

Rising health care expenditures can have several practical reasons. Very well described in Peter R. Koengsvedt's book about Managed Health Care, there are certain interrelations between the determinants 'demand' and 'supply' and between health care practice, politics and customer demands which are outlined in the following chapter.

The basic principle working on each market is: Increased demand leads to a relative increase of prices or to a relative decrease depending on the supply, the number of competing services. Additionally, the delivery of service may fluctuate corresponding to the respective providers like specialty clinics, nursing homes or the singular physicians seeing profit opportunities in times of scarcity or looking for saving possibilities in times of plenty. Both factors effect the total expenditures in the medical care sector. For example, the demand for medical service was high in 1965 through Medicare and Medicaid covering a lot of health service which weren't covered before. This lead to an increase in the relative price as well as the quantity of services because many providers have seen more profit chances than before. However, this situation can have a self-containing effect on the patient's demand, the physician's decision for treatment, and on the price level and quantity of services. Patients are not requesting service, if it is too expensive and physicians may face difficulties in getting sufficient reimbursement to cover their costs on the health supplies market.[6]

But why do prices rise, if the market forces generally prevent such a development through their self-balancing character?
This might be due to the kind of product health service is. Health is a meritorious good and therefore, the market principle of opposing and self-balancing demand and supply forces does not apply.

3.2.1 Health as a "Meritorious Good"

Merit(orious) good is an expression from the modern political economy describing a special kind of good between individual and public (or collective) goods. These goods are given to certain consignees without the normal monetary compensation and independently from their respective socioeconomic status. It is a provision, which is based on the normative social agreement. Without the sponsored provision of this good, the potential consumer might not pay for his health because of general monetary scarcity and/or the subjective opinion, there are more valuable goods on the market to spent the available money.
A reason for such normative social agreement which provide certain groups with sponsored products without the certainty of direct compensation can be seen in the use for the whole society: Social satisfaction of needs may prevent social unrest. Besides, healthy workers and employees are supposed to contribute more efficiently to a higher GDP. Such advantages make governments become interested in a partial dissociation from sole market-driven system ensuring health care for all people. However, this provision of care can contribute to rising expenditures, because it is resulting in a flow of money into the system. Providers are interested to receive that money by either lifting up the prices or offering new services.
Having stated the facts about the health care expenditures and theoretic reasons now form the basis on which I can thus describe why certain administrations focused on regulation in the 1960s while others focused on reinventing market forces in the 1980s in order to cut health care costs.

3.3 Cost Containment and Planning of Health Care

During the 1960s and 1970s hospitals made politicians become concerned because of the hospitals' contribution to rising national health care expenditures without highly improved access to care for the average population. To name a few examples: Excessive duplication of expensive facilities and services, rapid inflation of hospitals costs, wide variations in costs for similar services between hospitals, and the failure to substitute care in less costly settings even if that would be medically possible.
In the 1970s, one approach was taken to fight back these developments through regulation. A different way would be to rely on market forces and remove all legislative roadblocks which will be discussed later in the book, when a look on the 1980s and 1990s will be taken. Main reasons for regulation as method are:

1.) Inefficiencies in medical care demand: Patients often don't know which treatment is good for their health if they were only subject to a market system.
2.) Supply inefficiencies: These are mostly duplication of expensive services in economies of scale, excess of beds in communities and lack of provider incentives to be efficient.
3.) Increases in governmental expenditures on medical care. Political administrations are facing the dilemma of primarily having to contain the total dollar amounts while on the other hand efficiency of services have to be improved. Therefore they have to choose between two different rather unpopular ways: 1.) Raising taxes, or 2.) cutting back and planning health care by regulation.
4.) Lack of overall sufficient access to care: There are still many people, especially in rural or ghetto areas, with insufficient health care resources. Health care is still a scarce good in the States and without centrally planned distribution access would be inequitable.

What are the results of solving these problems by regulation?

Hospital regulation has a tight relation with hospital planning. A good example of this is the already mentioned governmental action on hospital development, the Hill-Burton-Act of 1946: It was mainly planned to improve expanded hospital construction financed with governmental funds after approval.

Hill-Burton and following voluntary attempts of regulation primarily aimed at regulating hospital investment and at broadening the equal coverage of the population, but had actually no effect with regard this goal. There was no significant difference in the increase of facilities and costs between planned and unplanned areas after voluntary planning agencies on the local level had started to work. They did not have any authority to approve or disapprove of hospital investment because of there voluntary status.[7]

The focus switched from capital investment controls to cost containment efforts after the enactment of Medicare and Medicaid and the flow of money through rising insurance coverage. Time was high for restrictive laws to cut the increase in private public expenditures.

3.4 Restrictive Planning

A major example for these restrictive planning laws were the Certificate-of-Need programs (CON). Between the years 1965 and 1973, 22 States passed this new legislation of hospital investment restriction. CON was covering an entire State and all existing facilities. If an already existing facility wanted to expand the service range or hospital beds or wanted to invest money in new construction the the certificate of need was necessary.

The bottom-line for this approval or disapproval was the need based on existing services and population e.g. within a special community. Except of Louisiana which never had a CON program, all States followed this approach sooner or later up to the eighties when the political attitudes according regulation changed.[8] CON legislation did not target the method of hospital reimbursement and patient or physician behavior. This is one of the reasons why it did fail in the end: Expenditures still rose. Other ways of regulation had to be pursued.

This approach represents the practice of the 'theory of regulation'. Under this traditional view of regulation, the governmental interest is to control costs. Actually, health care providers could try to misuse the regulatory approaches not to let governmental investment decrease. How could that approach eventually look like?

A second – the economical – theory of regulation applies to that case. This theory generally attributes a strong interest to misuse regulative legislation to the health care industry in keeping new competitors out of an already existing market. Existing industries prefer steady margins, but that does not apply to new competitors. Since CON did not target the expenditures directly like later rate regulation, existing facilities could increase their revenues without any danger. CON helped to make facilities safe by blocking new competitors. Allied with originally competing but also CON-regulated and existing facilities, they could built up cartels to design their desired price – a monopoly – structure.

The average price for services was expected to be higher than under a free market, where new competitors tried to enter this market by undercutting their (monopoly-) structure. This could happen, when there was a high competition between political parties and interest groups within one State. Every group is interested in political support like funds, votes, etc. Thus they get this support from the hospital industry as long they protect this industry closing the market, and even, if monopoly-pricing is not any party's desire.[9]

Subsequently, CON could be an explanation for higher overall expenditures or ineffectiveness in cost containment by hindering innovation through up-to-date facilities. Another regulatory approaches was 'rate regulation'

3.5 Rate Regulation

The movement towards a fixed-price payment system is a more direct method than entry controls for preventing excess capacity. The advantages of this method can be found in its innovative potential and in not holding the communities responsible to keep inefficient hospitals open or to be depending on cartels pushing up average prices. If hospitals do not compete against competitors entering the open market (vs. closed market under CON), and if they do not attract enough patients to fill existing facilities, they would have to close these facilities or they have to merge with potential competitors under a fixed-price system. In order to break all mentioned negative outcomes of capacity regulation, rate regulation was used to cope with the problem of costs. The implementation of Diagnosis Related Groups (DRG) is a good example of fixed-price-systems and 1970 health policies. Rate regulation was an idea targeting the actual prices for health services.
In 1983, the Federal Government then introduced these 'DRGs', a form of rate regulation. Fixed prices were paid for services of hospitalized Medicare patients.

The principle of the DRGs is the following: medical service at the level of output shall be delivered internally efficient on the least level of input. An example of this can be the technical equipment or the labor force. Further the external 'system' of service delivery shall be used efficiently within a community. The entire group of providers shall become interested in working and using resources together to achieve the minimum costs. Additionally it has to be proved, if hospitals substitute settings are there to provide the same service on a lower cost level.
DRG functions by setting up average prices for certain services or groups of patients within an area. This method to classify groups of illnesses and treatments has diverse implications listed as follows:

- Often patients have multiple diagnoses: Thus patients are mostly treated only for one disease or the physician has losses when applying treatments not covered in the diagnosis group. Therefore, the physician may chose the higher paid diagnosis.

- Also, the DRG classifications do not include scales for the severity of the patient's illness. As a consequence providers caring for a high number of severely sick patients are disproportionally hit and could try not to serve these patients. A way for a provider to get only profitable DRGs, can be non-price competition. The respective profitable patients are getting more service at the same price. These particular consequences contributed to the overall rise of health care costs.

3.6 Competition in Care Delivery

In this study, DRGs as a method of rate regulation were pointed out first because this measure takes a middle position between regulation and market. It was implemented and directed by the government, but there was a market in the sense that only those providers stayed alive that worked efficiently, and that no provider was hindered from opening facilities and to compete on a given reimbursement rate with existing health care providers.

The next step towards competition was done in the years of the Reagan Administration. Free market ideas were growing within the society, the general mentality primarily influenced the private sector to start unregulated competition to control rising health care expenditures. This private initiative was a result of the changed insurance situation in the states. Two-thirds had private insurance coverage - mostly purchased through the employer. The pressure to fight back rising costs now came from the consumers or the private insurance companies.
Apart from the increased power of the insurance sector, there were federally influenced initiatives and legislative events that provided the necessary preconditions of market competition before the 1980s. The most important initiatives and methods chosen besides the already described DRGs were:

- An increased supply of physicians resulting from the general demand for health care service provision and the demand for medical education for

American students instead of attracting foreigners since World War II in general and specifically from the governmental answer to that demand: the enactment of the Health Professions Assistance Act in 1963. By 1980, the number of physicians so rose to 200 per 100000 of population, by 1990, 232 per 100000.

This increased supply led to increased competition and lower consumer prices.

- The next event was the HMO-Act in 1973. Its goal was to use the already developed idea of prepaid health plans like the Kaiser Foundation Health Plan since the 1930s. The renamed health maintenance organizations adopted this idea and followed the incentive to make money depending on the efficient delivery of the market product 'health' for an annual capitation fee. 1979 A CON-amendment also let HMOs became less restricted.
- Further legislative changes towards competition were the elimination of free choice of the provider through the respective patients themselves under Medicaid. In 1981, it was decided that the States should take the chance to select the most efficient providers by negotiating contracts with them on behalf of the indigent population.
- Insurance companies adapted their benefit packages for employees of the diverse businesses: Lower-cost substitutes covering the same service – instead of any hospital – got the offer to provide the respective service, e.g. outpatient surgery. The reason was that employers and insurance companies became more interested in cost containment before.
- Excess capacity arose in the hospital market through the critical approach of utilization reviews and the use of inefficient or too costly institutions.
- Excess capacity in the health service area decreased because of a mentality change through a recession in the American economy: Health care providers became more convinced to adapt to alternative delivery systems in the 1980s.

3.6.1 Anti-trust-laws and Advertising

Market forces only influence the cost development negatively in combination with anti-trust-laws. If cartels are destroyed by law, the plan to behave anti-competitively is brought to suit. But those anti-trust-laws would have to result in a second step: Allowing the now really free-standing and competing providers to advertise how efficiently, successfully and cost-savingly they work to attract customers – the basis to stay alive in the new market environment.

- Anti-trust-laws: The Federal Trade Commission (FTC) was enacting anti-trust laws in the health field in 1975. These FTC-rulings were confirmed by the Supreme Court in 1982. From then onwards, boycotts, price fixing, etc. were brought to court.[10]
- Advertising: This is the necessary prerequisite for a functioning market. Having to compete with other providers, advertising gives important information about the medical services [price, quality and accessibility) and is the only way to attract customers. The existing fear in the field of the merit good 'health' that the patient might buy health service they do not need or harm was defeated. Advertising effected the market competition and prices in the health care system positively. As shown by a study of optometrics in 1963 and similar in 1970, prices were about 20% higher in states permitting advertising than in those not permitting advertising.[11] In 1982, the latter were repelled by the Supreme Court.

However, despite the desired and study-founded outcomes of free market forces onto prices health care costs are – even not as strong as in the 1960s and 1970s – still growing. Possible explanations are the willingness or demand for life-enhancing technology and the services for the increased population of the elderly and Medicare-recipients, the broadened offering of employment-based services. The rising gross domestic product over the years resulted in a flow of money into the health care system and in an increase in service supply.[12]

3.7 Overall View onto Health Care in the 20th Century

From the Hill-Burton-Construction Act in 1946 to the present, the power and responsibility shifted in accordance with the shift in target fields for health care policies: The 1960s were the decade of improving health care coverage of the population. In the 1970s, access to care was most important. It was the decade of CON.

Then in the 1980s under Reagan, market forces were seen to redeem the health care system from problems which had especially existed under CON like the lack of innovation.

In the 1990s, the election of Clinton let some people hope to solve still existing problems like insufficient access to care. Main issues in the 1990s were:

1.) National health insurance was to fight back the still high number of the uninsured or underinsured, especially in case of the needy, blind, disabled and aged people.
2.) Prevention was also seen as way to contain costs.
3.) A general new perspective on the biophysical environment and the individual behavior (reduction of environmental hazards, training non-self-indulgent, health endangering behavior) in order to reduce overall health expenditures.

However, the idea of a national health insurance did find some but not sufficient political support within the parties and the population. It failed in 1994. As before, only vulnerable groups within the society were covered by subsidiary programs. These three initiatives/tendencies – national health insurance, prevention and environmental and behavioral aspects – had in common that their center point was located on the local or state level. On one hand there was a sociological shift towards individual responsibility, on the treatment of the dramatically increased number of patients suffering from AIDS (Acquired Immunodeficiency Syndrome). Campaigns against the spreading of AIDS were mostly started on the level where it happened; this is in the local communities and their hospitals. A largely effected Medicaid population let the according state agency to deal with that problem. Consequences consisted in redefining optional benefits of governmental health plans, covering less persons under Medicaid and reducing the reimbursement rates for health professionals providing service to Medicaid recipients.[13]

Cutting back costs, however, is still a print paramount. The Balanced Budget Act (BBA) to cut back governmental spending for health care is an example that will be discussed combined with MGHS's business strategy later on in the book.

---

[1] See Wilson, F. A. and Neuhauser, D. (1982). *Health Services in the United States*. Page 120.

[2] Health Care Financing Administration (2000). *National Health Expenditures Projections, Table 1.*

[3] Health Care Financing Administration (2000). Office of the Actuary, National Health Statistics Group, *National Health Expenditures, Table 2.*

[4] Health Care Financing Administration (2000). Office of the Actuary, National Health Statistics Group, *National Health Expenditures..., Percent Distribution, Table 1.*

[5] Health Care Financing Administration (2000). Office of the Actuary, National Health Statistics Group, National Health Expenditures, Table 4.

[6] See Koengstvedt, Peter R. (1996). *The Managed Health Care Handbook.* Figure 3-1, Page 38 and text page 33 pp. Most of this quote following pages is based on this source.

[7] See May, J. in Havighurst, C. (1974). *Regulating Health Facilities Construction.*

[8] See Leeds, H. S. (1996). *Certificate of Need: Up for revision.*

[9] A study revealed, that those governmental relations - like campaign-financing - by these interest groups on behalf of the hospitals worked out in form of voting behavior of congress representatives against cost containment legislation. See Feinstein, P. J. and Melnick, G. A. (1984). *Congressional Voting Behavior on Hospital Legislation.*

[10] See following reviews about Anti-trust-laws and competition in the health care field: Costillo, L. B. (1985). *Anti-trust Enforcement in Health Care*; Leibenluft, R. F. and Pollard, M. R. (1981) *Anti-Trust Scrutiny of the Health Professions*; Havighurst, C. C. (1980) *Anti-trust enforcement in the Medical Services Industry,* and Learner A. N. (1984). *Federal Trade Commission Anti-Trust Activities in the Health Care Services Field.* Page 205-224.

[11] Benham, L. and A. (1972). *Regulating through the Professions.*

[12] Closing citation regarding Koengstvedt, Peter R. (1996). *The Managed Health Care Handbook.*

[13] Leichter, H. M. (1997). *Health Care Policy Reform in America: Innovations from the States.* Page 19-21.

4 Michigan, Marquette and its General Hospital

4.1 The State of Michigan

The State's capitol is Lansing. This city in the Lower Peninsula is the location of the government, diverse institutions of the public, the governmental-related private sector or interest groups, for example the Michigan Hospital Association (MHA). In the 1990s, the State was (and still is in 2000) governed by a Republican leadership.

Michigan is politically divided into 83 counties. The 10 most populated cities are Detroit, Grand Rapids, Warren, Flint, Lansing, Sterling Heights, Ann Arbor, Livonia, Dearborn and Westland. These metropolitan areas are located in the lower of the two peninsulas. With its total population rate, Michigan ranked in 1990 (9,295,287 residents) as also in 1998 (9,817,242 residents) 8th in the nation. Michigan has a low population density: In 1990, 163.6 and in 1998, 173 persons lived within a square mile. This average rate, however, differs very much from the higher populated Lower to the Upper Peninsula which is less populated. The three largest income producing industries in the state are manufacturing, tourism and agriculture. The larger Detroit area in the Lower Peninsula is the location for the nation's leading production of passenger cars and assembled trucks (General Motors, Ford, DaimlerChrysler). Looking on the Gross State Product of 1996, manufacturing was the largest industry with 28 percent, followed by the service industry with 17.6 percent, finance, insurance and real estate with 14.9 percent and retail trade with 9.4 percent.[1]
Michigan has a total wage and salary employment of 4,476,000 persons with 967,000 in manufacturing, 177,000 in mining and construction, 2,665,000 in private service and 668,000 in governmental service.
For the Upper Peninsula the numbers are 127,900 in total, there from 16,100 in manufacturing, 7,100 in mining and construction, 65,500 in service (private) and 39,200 in service (governmental). Wage and salary employment numbers were not available for proprietors, farming and other employment forms, they have to be added. Unemployment rates decreased taking into account January 1996 and

January 2000 in Michigan from 5.8 percent to 4 percent[2] (compared with the Upper Peninsula, the rate decreased from 10.6 percent to 7.6 percent, in Marquette County from 8.5 percent to 6 percent).[3]

Despite concentrated industrial regions in the south of Michigan, 53% of the country is forested land and 3, 288 miles of coastline – only the State of Alaska has more of this – due to the location of Michigan's two peninsulas between three of the Great Lakes: Lake Superior in the North, Lake Ontario in the East and Lake Michigan in the West. These natural attractions makes Michigan a vacation destination.

4.2 The Upper Peninsula and Marquette County

The Upper Peninsula (U.P.) of Michigan is a rural non-metropolitan area divided into 15 counties and has a population of approximately 320,000 residents. The 10 largest cities (each under 30,000 residents) are Marquette (23,336), Sault Ste. Marie (14,448), Escanaba (13,659), Menominee (10,099), Iron Mountain (8, 525), Ironwood (7,551), Houghton (7,498) and Ishpeming (7,292), Kingsford (5,290) and Negaunee (4,918).[4]

The County of Marquette, located on the shores of the Lake Superior had with 62,017 as for 1996 the highest number of population within the U.P. steadily decreasing since the early 1980s, where it still had 74,101 residents. In the history iron was the main reason, that drew settlers into this region, as shown in several city names (Iron Mountain e.g.). In 1919 iron-ore production hit its peak, in 1929 still 16 mines and today still two mines are operating in the county.
The city area got the name 'Marquette' around 1850 (Father Jaques Marquette, a Roman-Catholic priest and a missionary exploring large areas of the Upper Midwest, was the city's namesake). The first settlers beside the native Americans were descendants of Finnish and Scandinavian, French, Italian, Irish people and a few Germans.[5]
What about the decisive industrial and cultural areas of activity in the present?

Besides the mining and related construction industry, Marquette County was a location for a U.S. Army Air Force base up to the 1990s. The former Air Force base is now providing ground for new industrial establishments. The County of Marquette is home of Northern Michigan University and the Nation's third Olympic training center, the County Court in the City of Marquette. Marquette County is also stamped by a relative large health care industry, diverse smaller manufacturers and numerous retail and service businesses.[6]

This later diversification of the industrial sector had provided Marquette County and especially the City of Marquette with the ability to stay alive as a city over 150 years since it was founded. Lumber, iron ore and shipping were - as already mentioned - the basis on which Marquette grew in the early times. However, the "volatility of the markets for extractive industries" made responses necessary and so "brownstone quarrying, railroading, specialized heavy manufacturing, and the Air Force base have not always endured. Marquette, unlike other lumbering and mining towns and cities in the Upper Peninsula and the rest of the Midwest, has continued to move onward and upward.

Table 1 **Marquette County's 10 Largest Employers**
Marquette General Hospital[a], Marquette (2042): Health care service
Northern Michigan University, Marquette (1110): Education
Empire Iron Mining Partnership, Palmer (1000): Iron ore mining
Tilden Magnetide Partnership, Ishpeming (800): Iron ores
Michigan Dept. of Corrections, Marquette (456): Correctional institution
City of Marquette, Marquette (270): Executive offices
Simmons Airlines Inc., Negaunee (245): Air transportation[b]
Marquette County, Marquette (240): Executive offices
Wisconsin Electric Power Company, Marquette (240): Electric services
Kmart Corporation, Marquette (200): Department store

Nowadays, the industrial setting shows, that "the basis of the city's sustainability are the industries, that meet needs – education, health care and correction"[7]

[a] By this not the entire health system since 1999 is meant, only the Marquette based hospital facility.

[b] Since 1999 Marquette County has a new County Airport which rank as also the new rank of Simmons is not included in this listing and the available data yet.

Additionally, the tourism industry is worth being mentioned: The geographical setting is the basis on which diverse tourists' desire for natural beauty or seasonal attractions, like the Indian Summer e.g., are supposed to be satisfied.

The severe weather conditions with a lot of snow (lake-effect) in the winter are also a decisive factor for Upper Peninsula businesses, making this area – except of maybe Alaska – different from other U.S. regions. Specific data points out these conditions in the Marquette area:

- The average minimum temperature in January is 2F/-17C and in July 53F/12C;
- The average maximum temperature is in January 19F/-7C and in July 76F/24C;
- The precipitated average annual rainfall is 35 inch/89cm and average annual snowfall is 131 inch/333cm;
- There are on average three days a year with a temperatures above 90F/32C and 40 days below 0F/-18C.[8]

Being surrounded by spacious nature - large woods, many lakes and rivers - on the one hand promotes the tourism industry mainly in the summer, but on the other hand, isolates Marquette County and its businesses to a certain extend from other economically important areas in Michigan, the neighboring States Ohio, Indiana, Illinois and Wisconsin, or Canada in the north of the border.

Table 2 Marquette's Distance to Selected U.S. Metropolitan Areas

Chicago, Illinois: 370 miles (595 km)
Detroit, Michigan: 450 miles (724 km)
Lansing, Michigan: 390 miles (627 km)
Milwaukee, Wisconsin: 250 miles (402 km)
Minneapolis, Minnesota: 395 miles (635 km)

Marquette County and the Upper Peninsula are a mostly rural environment despite some larger towns between 5000 and 20,000 residents. These areas are facing several general problems which are also affecting the health status and health care access of the population in these areas.
Following statements can be made generally characterizing U.S. rural areas and supposed to be also right for the Upper Peninsula:

- Rural areas have higher rates of poverty than urban areas
- Rural areas still have a higher percentage of small business economies than urban areas. Low wages and smaller business size in rural areas also mean, rural residents have lower rates of employer based health insurance coverage
- Rural communities have less health and social services infrastructure
- The providers and clinics that provide care in rural areas often lack the resources available in many urban areas (out-stationing of workers, benefit counseling, and coordination between programs is more difficult)[9]

These are indicators shortly giving an outline about the surrounding setting, where MGHS is located and factors that might have an impact onto MGHS business areas. When taking a deeper look at the strategic plan of MGHS from 1996 further data, more specifically data related to MGHS' business goals and according strategy will be added.

4.3 Short Facts about Marquette General Hospital

At first, a short time line shall introduce into the institutional history of Marquette General Hospital. Additionally the institutional situation before and after strategic planning within 1990s will be pointed out. This is not meant to anticipate any interesting later results of this thesis, but this done in order to provide the reader with a frame. Further in the book, the particularities of the frame comprising the strategic planning process will be discussed.

4.3.1 History and Development of Marquette General Hospital

In July 1973, the history of Marquette General Hospital as today's entity began through the merging of two Marquette community hospitals – St. Luke's, opened in 1891 and St. Mary's, built in 1915.[10] Both facilities used to employ 40 physicians and 660 workers, the total annual payroll was about $3.6 million. After the merging, the new hospital was steadily growing, establishing new departments, services, procedures and pushing up the amount of annual revenues. The highlights of the developments within the 1970s, 1980s and 1990s were:

- The foundation of a 24-hour-staffed emergency department, a newly established Neonatal Intensive Care Unit, both in 1974;
- Opening of a Cardiac Catheter Laboratory in 1977;
- Performance of the first open-heart-surgery in 1978;
- The county' first emergency service system was built after taking over the city's ambulance service, also a Computer Tomography scanner (CT) was started to run in 1979;
- The establishment of a cancer program parallel to receiving a Certificate of Need for a linear accelerator[a] plus efforts to become the regional referral center for the Upper Peninsula in 1982, the taking over of the Family Practice Program at MGH in 1984 training rural primary care physicians;
- Foundation of an outreach clinic in Kingsford in 1986;
- Top-ranking in nation acquiring magnetic resonance therapy (MRI) establishing an MRI addition in 1987;
- Purchasing Ice Lake Clinic, Iron River in 1989 and Doctors Park, Escanaba in 1990;
- Opening of a second cardiac catheterization unit in 1991;
- Taking over Northern Home Health in 1992. In addition, psychiatric and rehabilitation programs were expanded.

---

[a] See also the review of U.S. health care legislation (CON) in the third chapter. In the late 1990s Michigan was still under CON legislation.

These developments were accompanied by three major expansion projects changing the face of the hospital buildings. Apart from this, the hospital was successful in recruiting new medical professionals to expand their specialties, e.g. in cardiac treatment or neurosurgery. Furthermore, the hospital developed two-way connections to the community and customers by establishing the Regional Advisory Board in 1994 or founding a cooperative network, the Upper Peninsula Health Care Network (UPHCN) together with 14 other hospitals within the Upper Peninsula in 1995 (See appendix for details.) Up to 1996 the number of employees reached about 2400 and more then 200 physicians on staff. The annual payroll was about $70 million.[11]

Up to 1996, Marquette General Hospital became the Upper Peninsula Regional Medical Center[a]. MGH is licensed by the Michigan Department of Public Health and the Department of Mental Health, and accredited by the Joint Commission on Accreditation of Healthcare Organizations (JCAHO) and the American College of Surgeons (ACS)[b].

In 1996, MGH was a 400-bed specialty care facility; besides being a community hospital for Marquette County providing primary care for local residents.[12]

[a] Regional Medical Center is a classification for being a referral center as also an institutional name of the "Upper Peninsula Medical Center" partly owned by MGHS offering space for doctors' offices

[b] The American College of Surgeons - founded 1913 - was promoting hospital standardization (tracking patients determining their treatment's effectiveness, minimum standards for hospital-care proofed through on-site inspections). In 1951 the Joint Commission on Accreditation of Hospitals, the predecessor of today's JCAHO, was established by the ACS, the AMA, the Canadian Hospital Association, the AHA, to improve the quality of medical care provided to the public. Since the Medicare Act of 1965, hospitals had to be compliant with JCAHO standards to receive governmental reimbursements. Electronic Source: http://www.jcaho.org.html [08/03/99 11:33]

In 1996 there were 44 specialties and subspecialties at MGH. Listed in alphabetical order:

- Addiction Medicine, Allergy, Anesthesiology
- Cardiology, Cardiac Electrophysiology Cardiovascular-Thoracic Surgery, Child and Adolescent Psychiatry, Clinical, Critical Care Medicine
- Dermatology
- Emergency Medicine
- Family Practice
- Gastroenterology, General Surgery, Geriatrics, Gynecology
- Hematology
- Infectious Disease, Internal Medicine
- Medical Toxicology
- Neonatology, Nephrology, Neurology, Neuroradiology, Neurosurgery
- Obstetrics, Occupational Medicine, , Oncology, Ophthalmology, Oral-Maxillofacial Surgery, Orthopaedics, Otolaryngology
- Pathology, Pediatrics, Pediatric Cardiology, Physical Medicine & Rehabilitation [Physiatry], Plastic & Reconstructive Medicine, Podiatry, Psychiatry
- Radiology, Radiation Oncology, Respiratory Medicine, Rheumatology
- Sports Medicine
- Urology[13]

In addition, Marquette General Hospital became home to "the Upper Michigan Heart Institute, the Upper Michigan Centers for Neuroscience, Rehabilitation and Cancer Treatment; the Upper Michigan Behavioral Health Service, the Upper Michigan Wellness Institute, the Women's and Children's Center, and Family Care Doctors."[14]

Worth mentioning are the application of up-to-date fiberoptic, microscopic, laser and laparoscopic, and video surgical technologies in medical treatment. MGH got into telemedicine and teleradiology already before 1996. Additional to the regular health service of MGH, the new home health service let approximately 11,000 inpatients and 200,000 outpatients a year receive care. Another corner-stone of MGH in 1996 was MGH's position as a teaching facility. In the following the diverse educational pathways and the affiliations of Marquette General are given.

- Family Practice Residency Program (Michigan State University)
- Nursing (Northern Michigan University, Bay de Noc Community College, Gogebic Community College)
- Physician Assistants (Wayne State University, Mercy College of Detroit, Western Michigan University)
- Physical Therapy (Wayne State University, University of Michigan, College of St. Scholastica, Oakland University, Grand Valley State College)
- Occupational Therapy (Eastern Michigan University)
- School of Radiography (Northern Michigan University)
- Laboratory (Northern Michigan University) [15]

Condensing MGH's strategic efforts before 1996, there have to be named:
1.) The expansion regarding facilities, services, technology, recruiting specialty physicians;
2.) The search for cooperative networks with the community and other providers and;
3.) Developing the strengths MGH as a regional referral center: owning or networking with clinics throughout the Upper Peninsula.

4.3.2 System Development – From MGH to MGHS

In 1999, MGH looked different. Not only the name was changed from Marquette General Hospital to Marquette General Health System, this name-change also stands for a new institutional setting. Because of the common historic background of two community hospitals, both church affiliated, MGH provided sole community care. After merging and broadening the range of service provision to the entire Upper Peninsula by establishing clinics and building referral networks, can be seen as a tendency from a individual hospital facility toward a system. Marquette General Health System was providing more different services, covering more customer groups and so reaching higher patient rates. The 1999 data compared with the 1996 data shows this. After adding adding new services, MGHS had 52 specialties. The new ones are listed below:

- Addiction Psychiatry additionally to Addiction Medicine
- Geriatric Psychiatry additionally to General Geriatry
- Hand Surgery and Vascular Surgery additionally to existing surgery specialties
- Nuclear Cardiology additionally to General Cardiology and
- Pain Management

The affiliations with the diverse educational facilities were kept. Another expansion project regarding additional room for specialties took place in 1999. The number of inpatients remained stable at 11,000, the amount of outpatients increased about 220,000 to 420,000 a year corresponding with another fact, the operation of clinics in nine communities. The number of inpatient-beds was lowered to 360 beds. The amount of employees (2400) and physicians on staff (200) stayed stable over the time.[16]

The provider network of MGH as for 1999 includes the main facility, nine extra-specialty groups of Medical Associates, home health and hospice ventures in five communities and an affiliation with and partial ownership of the Peninsula Medical Center (Office and Practice space rented by physicians), the newly founded assisted living venture in Marquette and the Upper Peninsula Health Plan (UPHP), an insurance plan for U.P. residents. For location of facilities see map in appendix.

4.3.3 Management, Financial Situation and Status

The hospital's organizational chart as for 1999 (see also appendix) has four levels of authority (here from high to low):

1.) The Board of Trustees[a] consisting of 15 members including one president,
2.) The Chief of the Medical Staff, the Hospital Auxiliary, the Regional Advisory Board and the Chief Executive Officer,
3.) Five Assistant Administrators including the Chief Finance Officer and
4.) 44 Department Heads including Program Directors.[17]

In a last step, the financial or revenue side of MGH within the Upper Peninsula shall be pointed out by giving the sources of gross patient revenues. The kind of payers and the kind of customer play a decisive role in strategic planning at Marquette General Hospital.
Depending on governmental reimbursement – over 50 percent through Medicare plus Medicaid – made MGH a so called 'Disproportional Share Hospital (DSH)'. That has to do with the hospital's non-profit status. This status exempts a private organization, like MGH or later MGHS Inc. from income taxes as ruled in the U.S. Internal Revenue Code. Further, nonprofit institution 'General Hospital' enjoy exemptions from diverse other State and local taxes; however, this depends on the service of this firm, which has to benefit the community.
"The margins earned by these providers are exclusively re-invested in programs and services, that meet the health care needs of the community.“ [18] This way of service is incorporated in the hospital mission.[19]

[a] A non-profit hospital is governed by a board of trustees whose members are from the surrounding community. The Board duties and responsibilities – as ruled in the bylaws of MGH – are to be aware of all projects to provide the residents with medical care as outlined in the mission, vision and value statement. All advices, plans and management decisions need final approval by the board with regard to their necessity and how those expenditures are financially covered. See also chapter nine.

Before 1996 and in 1999, the hospital had to deal with following revenue shares:

Table 3 MGH Gross Patient Revenue in Percent		
Sources	MGH 1994	MGHS 1999
Medicare	46.9	46.4
Medicaid	9.3	9.2
Blue Cross	18.6	23.8
Commercial insurance	16.9	13.3
Managed care	2.0	-------
Self-pay and other	6.3	0.9 and 6.4 [20]

To round off this short overview with regard to developments and attitudes of Marquette General Hospital before and at the end of the strategic planning phase between 1995 and 1999, the essence of the non-profit provider can be further characterized by giving MGH's mission, vision and values. They are representing the way MGH did business in the late 1990s.

MGH and later MGHS follows the mission to provide access to health service and improving the health status of Marquette Counties and the U.P.'s residents with no exclusion. (also in the case of uncompensated care for patients that are underinsured or uninsured). As a reminder, for giving that service to the community, MGHS as a non-profit provider is exempt of income taxes.
The vision was to put the mission in a frame of business ratio, that is to prosper, to work effectively and to do that in cooperation with other following (mission) goals.
Therefore, six values were defined to be met in the all-day business life: Competency, Customer Service, Quality, Safety, Stewardship, Teamwork (See appendix for details). These points give a rough picture, some anchor points of what is outlined in the next part of the thesis pointing out the theoretic strategic plan and examples of applied strategic management at MGH.

---

[1] See Michigan Information Center/Department of Management and Budget (April 30th 1999).

[2] See Michigan Department of Career Development/Employment Agency/Labor Market Analysis Section (2000). *Labor Market Data.*

[3] See Michigan Department of Career Development/Employment Agency (2000). *Labor Market Data.*

[4] Travel & Recreation Association (1999). *Michigan's Upper Peninsula.*

[5] See Downs, G. N. and M. C. (1999). *Marquette - Images of America.*

[6] Marquette County, Michigan (2000). *Information Site.*

[7] See Downs, G. N. and M. C. (1999). *Marquette - Images of America.*

[8] See Marquette County, Michigan (2000). *Information Site.*

[9] The Rural Work group of the Interagency Task Force on Children's Health Insurance Outreach (1999). *Why is rural important?*

[10] See Downs, G. N. and M. C. (1999). *Marquette - Images of America.* Page 42,43.

[11] See Marquette General Hospital, Community Relations and Marketing (February 1996). *Hotline*, and for mental health and rehab expansion see Moody's State Health Care Review (1995). *Michigan, Marquette General Hospital.* Page 82.

[12] Marquette General Hospital (September 1996). Information Folder.

[13] Marquette General Hospital (March 1996). *Friends & Neighbors Caring for You, the Services of Marquette General Hospital.*

[14] Marquette General Hospital. (September 1996). *Information Folder.*

[15] Marquette General Hospital. (September 1996). *Information Folder.*

[16] Marquette General Hospital (March 1999). *Information Folder.*

[17] Marquette General Hospital (1999). *Organizational Chart.*

[18] Michigan Health & Hospital Association (1998). *Hospital Community Benefits Survey.*

[19] Simon, J.G. (1987). *The treatment of nonprofit Organizations: A Review of Federal and State Policies.* Page 67-98.

[20] Marquette General Hospital (2000). *Fiscal Year 1999 CFO Finance Information.* [20] See Michigan Information Center/Department of Management and Budget (April 30th 1999).

[20] See Michigan Department of Career Development/Employment Agency/Labor Market Analysis Section (2000). *Labor Market Data.*

[20] See Michigan Department of Career Development/Employment Agency (2000). *Labor Market Data.*

[20] Travel & Recreation Association (1999). *Michigan's Upper Peninsula.*

[20] See Downs, G. N. and M. C. (1999). *Marquette - Images of America.*

[20] Marquette County, Michigan (2000). *Information Site.*

[20] See Downs, G. N. and M. C. (1999). *Marquette - Images of America.*

[20] See Marquette County, Michigan (2000). *Information Site.*

[20] The Rural Work group of the Interagency Task Force on Children's Health Insurance Outreach (1999). *Why is rural important?*

[20] See Downs, G. N. and M. C. (1999). *Marquette - Images of America.* Page 42,43.

[20] See Marquette General Hospital, Community Relations and Marketing (February 1996). *Hotline*, and for mental health and rehab expansion see Moody's State Health Care Review (1995). *Michigan, Marquette General Hospital.* Page 82.

[20] Marquette General Hospital (September 1996). Information Folder.

[20] Marquette General Hospital (March 1996). *Friends & Neighbors Caring for You, the Services of Marquette General Hospital.*

[20] Marquette General Hospital. (September 1996). *Information Folder.*

[20] Marquette General Hospital. (September 1996). *Information Folder.*

[20] Marquette General Hospital (March 1999). *Information Folder.*

[20] Marquette General Hospital (1999). *Organizational Chart.*

[20] Michigan Health & Hospital Association (1998). *Hospital Community Benefits Survey.*

[20] Simon, J.G. (1987). *The treatment of nonprofit Organizations: A Review of Federal and State Policies.* Page 67-98.

[20] Marquette General Hospital (2000). *Fiscal Year 1999 CFO Finance Information.*

5 Theoretic Foundations of Strategic Hospital Management

5.1 Introduction into Strategic Management

After giving a general introduction into the subject of this case study and its environment in the last chapters, the thematic perspective shall be explained. Therefore, the expression 'strategic management' and its theoretic foundation and ways to approach it scientifically will be described. The according steps within this process, the diverse variants of strategies and 'grand' strategies will be highlighted. Important neighboring fields of management-science as organizational behavior (OB) and systems theory will also be linked to strategic management in the health care environment. This introduction's goal is to provide the reader with the theoretical basis of strategic management before the MGH plan itself will be observed.

Table 4 Steps of Strategic Management

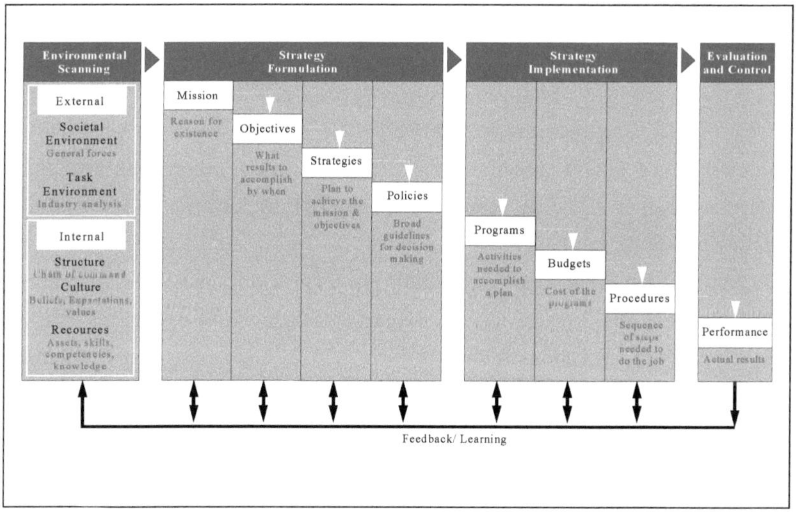

Source: Hunger, D. J. and Wheelen T. L. (1998). *Strategic Management and Business Policy.* Page 9

As defined by Wheelen and Hunger,

> "Strategic management is that set of managerial decisions and actions that determines the long-run performance of a corporation. It includes environmental scanning (both external and internal), strategy formulation (strategic or long-range planning) strategy implementation, and evaluation and control."

Strategic management was originally called business policy. Business policy had the function to link the various business activities of a firm and to form one direction of management. Strategic management "incorporates the integrative concerns of business policy with a heavier environmental and strategic emphasis."[1]
This theoretic approach to strategic management will be filled with substance later on in the book, identifying strengths, weaknesses, opportunities and threats of MGHS as seen by the consulting firm. Regarding the formulation of a strategy, there are several types of strategic plans:

- Short-range plans for a year or less;
- Intermediate-range plans for one up to two years and;
- Long-range plans for a period of five years or more.

According to Schermerhorn, Jr, "strategic plans address long-term needs and set comprehensive action directions for the entire organization and operational plans, sometimes called tactical plans ... [and] define what needs to be done to implement strategic plans."
Those operational plans are production plans (regarding methods and technology), financial plans (regarding the financial foundation of operations), facility plans (regarding buildings, material, layouts etc.), marketing plans (regarding the selling and distribution of goods) or human resource plans (regarding recruitment and placement of personnel).

Further, one can differ between the approaches taken to planning.

- Top-down planning defines the objectives and let lower levels develop plans within certain boundaries.
- Bottom-up planning takes the other direction, which plans are made without any constraints on the lower level and passed to the upper level.

On the one hand, top down is considered to be more clearly directed and not in jeopardy to be uncoordinated, on the other hand, bottom-up planning can lead to a better feeling of empowerment through commitment and ownership with regard to the ideas.[2]
However, if a plan circulates among all levels of staff, it can lead to the situation that for example "requests for additional space or objections to proposed changes, will have to be more fully justified and documented than would be other wise the case."[3] Thus advantages and disadvantages have to be considered thoroughly before deciding about the way of planning. Following Schermerhorn Jr, strategic planning develops strategies on three levels:

- Corporate strategies target the entire institution or firm and set the direction for the allocation of resources.
- Business strategies focus a single business unit or production line. For example, with regard to competition for customers in the respective service field. In single-business enterprises, business strategies correspond with corporate strategies.
- Functional strategies guide specific operations, like functions of marketing, research or human resource, etc.

At last management science identifies four groups of grand or master strategies within the process of strategy formulation:

- Growth strategies try to increase size and number of existing operations.
- Retrenchment or defensive strategies aim at improving performance and efficiency by downsizing or restructuring operations.
- Stability strategies apply, if a business is doing well and wants to maintain this status trying to prevent any major risks through changes.
- Combination strategies apply several of the other strategies at one time using one or more strategies in respective subsystems. A combinatory approach becomes necessary in complex organizations facing high competition or environmental changes.[4]

To prepare the basis of this review of Marquette General's strategic management additional theoretic building stones as organizational theory, organizational behavior, and systems theory are used. These theories cannot be left aside because they provide the reader with the necessary information about basic thoughts and the definition of diverse expressions used within the development of strategies within an institution like MGHS. Limits and boundaries to neighboring areas have to be set by clearly defining the respective expressions used for strategic planning. Later evaluation, interpretation and formulation of conclusions can be only done letting the reader know, what the authors of the strategic plan and the author of this thesis is talking about.

Organizational theory – a sociologically and psychologically based science – is targeting the behavior of organizations and groups of organizations to understand why and how people organize into (work) groups and how these groups function. Slightly different to this is organizational behavior – rooted in psychology. It is concerned with the behavior of individuals and groups of individuals in these organizations. So the direction of both research disciplines is the same, but the focus is different.

5.2 Organizational Theory – Key Terms for Strategic Planning

5.2.1 Structural Contingency Theory

Focusing the organizational structure with the major proposition that there is no 'best' organizational structure: The situation itself determines whether more or less centralized decision making will work best for factors such as size of organization and nature of environment. This theory emphasizes the impact of the external environment and the nature of the respective people on how organizations are set up and should function.

5.2.2 Resource Dependent Theory

This theory targets the relationship between organizations, stating, that organizations gain or lose power in relation to other organizations based on the resources they have and those they need. If an organization needs resources that another one has, the first one has less power and will behave in ways that will enable it to gain power. This theory emphasizes political processes and their impact on organizational decision making.

5.2.3 Institutional Theory

This theory's basic proposition is that organizational structure, functioning, and preferred outcomes are more heavily influenced by prevailing norms, values and beliefs – the areas of this theory's emphasis – than by perfectly rational processes, as factors such as desires to imitate other organizations believed to be good ones, to be seen as legitimate by more powerful actors, and to adhere to regulations and avoid sanctions all determine how organizations will actually behave. This theory emphasizes social and psychological processes. An example are 'gag rules' in some health care organizations. Hospitals don't want to have their health care professionals to tell patients all possibilities of treatment, although they are medically appropriate, because the payment of these procedures is not covered. In this case, managed care norms affected treatment policies, although there are no medical scientific rationales.[5]

5.3 Key Terms of Strategic Health Care Management

5.3.1 Systems

A system can be defined as an aggregate of multiple processes that interrelate and whose effects are dynamically depending on each other in that sense that a common effect is reached. A system can include sub-systems which can be relatively independent within the limits of the overall system. One can differ between open and closed systems. The most decisive feature of systems is the interdependence of all components, a tendency to keep the system balanced. Important functions of these systems in order to control themselves are allocation and integration of components and arrangement of these components within the environment or the mediation with it. The existing dynamic connection of all single parts and effects in a system can be seen as causal relation. The main difference of this systematic view to the mechanic causality in natural science (a single cause-effect relation) is, that all cause-effect relations interrelate with each other. [6]

5.3.2 Organizations

An organization is defined as a group of people who have joined together to accomplish goals they cannot achieveon their own. Work organizations had their initial phase in the industrialization when people with different backgrounds moved into cities and started new ways of achieving goals.[7] In a hospital, for example, people with diverse skills join together to provide comprehensive health service, whether it be in surgery, pediatrics, psychiatry, etc.

5.3.3 Institutions

In differentiation to organizations which are groups of people, institutions are defined as procedures that regulate behavior. Often however, the same definition as for organizations is used in a broader sense. Organizational behavior and the institutional theory shortly defined further below is useful to explain the specialty of some behavioral processes within hospitals and give clues on how to look at them.[8]

5.3.4 Integration and Differentiation

Integration is the degree to which specialized services or functions are coordinated across specialty lines. *Vertical integration* means in the United States that a single organization owns all types of health services necessary along a continuum (e.g. from primary care to hospital care to nursing care). Horizontal integration refers to clusters of the same type of institution owned by one organization. Differentiation is the extent to which an organization specializes in terms of the market (e.g. target population) it serves or the product or service it provides

5.3.5 Economies of Scale and Strategic Alliances

An economy of scale is an organization, large enough to negotiate favorable prices or contracts.

Strategic alliances are forms of interorganizational relationships which give organizations greater economies of scale while retaining their autonomy and individual ownership. Those linkages foster achievement of critical organizational goals.[9] Alliances are often a preferred strategy especially by nonprofit organizations. Those alliances are seen as a method to enhance their capacity to serve patients or to acquire resources while not losing their identity.[10] Besides alliances also mergers as a special kind of definite alliances are a potentially beneficial strategy helping to reduce costs by using resources more efficiently. In the 1980s more than 400 U.S. [nonprofit] hospitals were involved in mergers.[11]

5.3.6 Strategic Piggybacking

This term describes the development of a new activity for the not-for-profit organization that would generate the funds needed to make up the difference between revenues and expenses.[12] As revealed by a study of the U.S. General Accounting Office, the amount of income producing activities has significantly increased since the 1970s. Examples for such activities are nonprofit hospitals offering wellness programs or auxiliary services like book stores.[13] In what way MGH tries to gain additional income will be highlighted in the specific management plans of MGH for example in the area of finance described later on. However, these offerings can result in a potential drawback for the hospital in form of losing the tax-exempt status if the these services are "substantially related to the organization's exempt purposes, particularly if the income from the business exceeds approximately 20 percent of total organizational revenues."[14]

5.3.7 Organizational Behavior – Perspectives for Observation

Organizational behavior, in general, includes individual and group behavior in organizations. Organizational Behavior (OB) is also covering the way how job satisfaction and job performance are influenced by certain job designs. Further viewpoints of organizational behavior are the differences between several individuals doing work: for example, feelings, attitudes, talents, and contributions in work settings. People behave different, when they are working in groups than if they work alone. These topics could be focused on three overlapping levels:

- The individual level (personal characteristics as motivation)
- The group level (dynamic of work behavior as communication)
- The system level (which also overlaps with organizational theory issues, for example, organizational development and organizational culture)[15]

5.3.8 Three Key Points as Potential Foundation for Planning

- The workforce is changing with regard to diversity, skills and values through the different ethnic backgrounds, gender and age issues or different lifestyles.
- The customer expectations are changing. Quality, service and costs are customer needs that have to be met to stay in business. Total quality management has to be included in strategic management
- Organizations are changing. Triggering events and tendencies are the process of restructuring through a global economy's pressures on the national market or proceeding developments in technologies and information needs.
- Leader roles within management are changing. Coordinator, or perhaps coach or facilitator, makes a more apt description of the role of a manager.[16]

Listing these theories, key terms and propositions within the last paragraphs has not meant the intention to completely introduce all expressions and circumstances, organizational theory deals with. The goal of this entire chapter is to provide the reader the reader with a viewpoint how to look at MGH/MGHS in order to come to a scientific evaluation of the research findings of strategic management.

---

[1] See Hunger, D. J. and Wheelen T. L. (1998). *Strategic Management and Business Policy.* Page 9.

[2] See Schermerhorn, J. R. Jr. (1996). *Management and Organizational Behavior.* Page 66.

[3] Allen, R. W. (1976). *Hospital Planning Handbook.* Page 1.

[4] See Schermerhorn, J. R. Jr. (1996). *Management and Organizational Behavior.* Page 70-71.

[5] Lancaster, J. (1999). *Nursing Issues in Leading and Managing Change.* Page 96-98.

[6] See Bertalanffy (1972) in: Dorsch, F. (1994). *Psychologisches Woerterbuch (Psychological Dictionary).* Page 781.

[7] March, J.G. and Simon, H.A. (1958). *Organizations.*

[8] See Dorsch, F. (1994). *Lexikon der Psychologie (Psychological Dictionary).* Page 354, and Schmidt, M. G. (1995). Woerterbuch zur Politik (Political Dictionary). Page 428.

[9] See Lancaster, J. (1999). *Nursing Issues in Leading and Managing Change.* Page 104-112.

---

[10] See Provan, K.G. (1984). *Interorganizational Cooperation and Decision-Making Autonomy in a Consortium Multihospital System*. Page 494-504, and Luke R. D., Begun J. W. and Pointer D. D. (1989), *Quasi-Firms: Strategic Interorganizational Forms in the Health Care Industry*. Page 9-19.

[11] See Collins, S. (1993). *A Bitter Financial Pill.* Page 83-96.

[12] See Nielsen, R. P. (Summer 1982). *SMR Forum: Strategic Piggybacking – A Self-subsidizing Strategy for Nonprofit Insitutions*. Page 65-69.

[13] See Bacon, D.C. (April 1989). *Nonprofits Groups: An unfair edge? Nation's business*. Page 33-34.

[14] See Skloot, E. (1983). *Should Not-for-profits go into business?* Page 21.

[15] See Weinert (1998). *Organisationspsychologie (Organizational Psychology)*. Page 54.

[16] See Schermerhorn, J. R. Jr. (1996). *Management and Organizational Behavior*. Page 10.

6 Strategic Planning at MGH

6.1 Basic Situation of MGH in 1996

In June 1995 Moody's State Health Care Review published a report about Marquette General Hospital. It gives information on how further strategic planning has to look like, or which of the mentioned grand strategies to choose.
Moody is a rating agency evaluating the condition of firms, organizations and institutions like hospitals. They rate hospitals on an alphabetical scale. The rating has an impact on the value of MGH shares on the bond-market, where MGH is present. Selling bonds enables MGH to finance e.g. the construction of new or the renovation of old facilities. The rating of Moody's provides potential investors on the bond market with information, wether it will pay off to buy MGH bonds to borrow money to MGH. A good rating expresses the potential of MGH to do economically well at the moment and in the near future. That may result in an increasing bond-price, the chance for investors to make profit.
Marquette General Hospital received a positive rating, an 'A-rating' in 1995, just like in the ratings before in May 1989, May 1989 and February 1977. Despite the surrounding economy being rated as weak (see also chapter 4) there were following rationales for this rating:

- The status as sole community provider and regional referral center and the Upper Peninsula's only tertiary care provider;
- Efficient utilization of services and facilities over the foregone three years resulted in double digit increases in net patient revenues, and;
- A modest debt load and no immediate upcoming plans to borrow new money because of an improved liquidity position.[1]

In such a superior position - doing economically well - the strategy is supposed to contribute to maintain the status or even to improve it. The following summary and selected quotes of the strategic plan of MGH represents the way MGH should have taken between 1996 and 1999 in the eyes of consultants. Bearing these results in mind, it becomes interesting to look at the way the MGH administration actually took.

6.2 The Strategic Plan – Factor Analysis

In 1995, the hired consulting firm started analyzing the object. First, the external market, including the served patient base, population characteristics and key competitors were reviewed. Second, the internal resources were analyzed: utilization of services, financial performance, medical staff characteristics, and the operational productivity. Also, confidential interviews with physicians, community leaders, members of the governing board and management were made. These steps are reflecting the phase of environmental scanning. At the end of the analysis period, a report was conducted and strategies formulated.
How was the external environment of MGH viewed by the consulting experts?

6.2.1 The Diverse Challenges

The Upper Peninsula of Michigan would be offering chances in form of "a unique opportunity since it is a separate geographical area with enough population and resources to be able to build an integrated delivery system[a] without undo concern about external competitive threats."

However, MGH had to cope with certain challenges influencing its success and viability in the upcoming years of 1996 to 1999, as changes in the delivery of health care, increased regional competition, decreasing reimbursement and maintaining an adequate flow of patients. Because of the hospital's overall position being rated as healthy, the consulting firm concluded that strategic management had to answer the question: What does MGH need to continue to succeed in the years ahead?

---

[a] that means: organizationally separated hospitals, physicians, prepayment, ambulatory services and long-term care are combined in one organization, an integrated system. See also chapter 5

This represents the search for a stability strategy combined with one or more of the other major strategies like the growth strategy following the previously (before 1995) started process of expanding "beyond [the] traditional hospital role and to begin to think and to behave like an integrated delivery system." But why should MGH follow these demands? Which rationales are given by the consultants?

Changes in the Delivery of Health Care: At MGH, ambulatory service delivery increased since 1992 and the average length of stay declined at a rate of 16 percent. Outpatient services were seen to have large growth rates. The U.P. had 1993 and 1994 lower utilization of inpatient services than the States and Michigan.

Regional Competition and Decreasing Reimbursement: The existing hospitals within the U.P. and neighboring areas, like Wisconsin and Minnesota, were all seen to face tougher competition for patients to keep their services profitable. This increased competition – e.g. effected by managed care (see paragraphs below) – would also force providers to seek possibilities for collaboration to lower costs to stay in business.

Flow of Patients: According factors were the population growth, patient groups and the ratio of patient out-migration and in-migration. Overall population growth of 1.0 percent projected for 1995 to 2000 was expected to be slower than in the state of Michigan, which population was expected to grow by 2.1 percent. Marquette was supposed to have a decline of 108 people annually (0,2 percent). Especially the decrease in pediatric population was supposed to influence the patient flow negatively with 478 fewer children ages 14 and under and for all other U.P. counties with a total decline of 661 children. Women of childbearing years (age 15 to 44) were supposed to decline at a rate faster than in the state of Michigan.

On the other side the U.P. had a stable and significantly higher rate of older population base than the state of Michigan (16.5 percent of the U.P. population

would be age 65 and older). All projections were seen to be affected negatively by the recent closing of K.I. Sawyer Air Force Base. Besides the U.P. out-migration would affect the patient flow.
In 1994 15 percent of the population had chosen non-U.P. providers to receive health care despite MGH developing to the only tertiary care provider offering care for all health needs locally. However, 17 percent of all patients in 1994 were people not being residents of the U.P.

That is the overall view on Marquette General's business environment. The following factors describe the specifics explored by the consulting firm.

Regional Competition and Price Competition: Freestanding hospitals were supposed to appear most vulnerable, because even no crisis existed, a tendency toward "hospitals, physicians and other health care organizations joining together in various relationships .. [was] posing threats to freestanding hospital's viability." Competition on the local basis would be replaced by regional competition.[a] Apart from this, managed care organizations (and insurance companies) were supposed to have steady increases in the numbers subscribers, which are interested in costs containment. That is supposed to lead to tougher price competition. In 1995, only 2 percent of patient days of care within the U.P. were paid for by managed care organizations. Comparing this with the general higher rates of the U.S. with an average of 12 percent this was supposed to grow.

[a] Competition can be answered by lowering costs or increasing the stream of revenues to secure the own position. If the costs for services are decreasing through the containment efforts of insurance and managed care, another way is seeking for additional customers/patients. This was supposed to happen on a broader regional level instead the former community or county level also taking into account the higher willingness to cope with longer distances between patient and care provider expressed in the high average rate of out-migration.

Competition and Vertical Integration: Since the intensified competition would happen on a larger scale and regional basis, hospitals were forced to transform into systems.
"These systems ultimately would be vertically-integrated, in multiple locations, encompassing an area much greater than the present hospital service area and composed of interlocking arrangements between hospitals, primary care physicians, specialists, and managed care plans."

Shift of Financial Focus: The financial focus was expected to shift from a capital asset concern to one of increasing the stream of revenue according to the new era of competition. The stream of revenue then had to be increased with respect to the still existing weakness of the location of MGH in a rural environment with low population density and high patient out-migration. The subtotal of U.P. counties' patients was 6,040 in 1994. The U.P. percentages (plus Marquette County's 336 patients percentages) of persons leaving, were: 55.9 percent (65.2 percent) to Wisconsin hospitals, 28.5 percent (1.5 percent) to North Central Michigan Hospitals, 5.1 percent (17.9 percent) to South East Michigan Hospitals and 10.4 percent (15.5 percent) to other hospitals. All of the specialties, the patients were leaving the U.P. for were also offered at MGH.

Facilities Development: Despite MGH's up-to-date appearance and the new buildings, several important services stayed in older buildings, and newer buildings had significant vacancies at the same time because of a decline in inpatient behavioral health services. Therefore, future facility development had to be on the agenda paying attention to the demands of a changing healthcare environment.

Productivity Improvements: The hospital's internal ability to deliver health care more efficiently and more cost-effectively had to be kept and improved. Investors were not seen to have any incentive to invest capital without a hospital being concerned about improving productivity through "intelligent program design and care full staff education e.g." reacting to above mentioned changes.

Market Share: The market share of MGH for 1995 was the following: the hospital captured from Marquette County 72 percent of the patients who needed to be hospitalized and 50 percent of all of the patients. Out of the U.P. counties the numbers were: 25 percent of the hospitalized patients and 44.0 percent of all patients. The relatively high percentages of nearly 50 percent of all patients of the U.P. captured by MGH highlights how important it was for MGH to strategically focus the entire U.P.

People are not only out-migrating for care, they are also in-migrating. This can be strengthened through efforts to deliver care more efficiently via networks and vertical integration.

The overall inpatient market share of clinical groups with regard to U.P. discharges is 25 percent. Behavioral Health and Rehabilitation were two specialties, where MGH clearly dominated the U.P. market: 57 percent of patients needed to be hospitalized in Behavioral Health were captured by MGH and 77 percent for inpatient rehab care. Strategic thinking has to pay attention to the expected shift toward increased outpatient services in these specialties, to hold this rate. That means updated program design. In most surgical areas, MGH captured and overall rate of 27 percent of the U.P. market. The highest Upper Peninsula's market shares were reached by MGH in Surgery and Cardiovascular Medicine, Gynaecology, Pediatrics, General Medicine.

Medical Staff: MGH's medical staff was broad-balanced in several respect. In 1995, 29 percent of the 205 physicians were 'key physicians' accounting for 83 percent of the activity. Key physicians are the major admitters of patients. Mostly, the amount of key physicians was around 20 percent accounting for 80 percent of the activity.

26 percent of MGH's active and provisional staff and 27 percent of the 'key staff' were primary care physicians. The relative high share of the key staff was on the one hand contributing to a steady stream of revenue through referrals. On the other hand, this group of physicians may made it difficult for the administration to design management plans, that corresponded with the physician's sometimes conflicting needs. The relative low amount of primary care physicians, which can be seen as a consequence of the history of hospitals in the U.S. being

generally more specialty driven, could be a disadvantage for MGH if managed care plans played a more decisive role in the future which more focus 'primary care' than 'specialty care'.
Otherwise diverse specialty services were supposed to positively effect MGH by attracting patients that have free choice of the provider (understanding specialty treatment in the sense of top treatment). At last it can be seen as a strength (in the sense of commitment) that the medical staff is of young age: 48 percent of the active and provisional staff and 45 percent of the key staff was under 45 years old, 15 percent of the active and provisional and 11 percent of the 'key' staff was close to retirement.
The latter is describing one part of the economical situation of MGH in 1995. Following strengths, mentioned by physicians, community leaders, members of the governing board and the management, now complete the analysis.

- Marquette General Hospital was seen as an institution "comfortable with its delivery of high quality patient care, adequate patient population, and good financial health." MGH's operating margin 1992-95 was 2.8 percent the average total margin 3.9 percent. The state average was 2.4 percent and 3.1 percent.
- Providing all areas of health services, which were mentioned with regard to out-migration, MGH had a chance to recapture lost markets building up on above mentioned strength.
- A large proportion of key physicians (29 percent), the major admitters for the hospital account for 83 percent of the hospital's activity and ensuring the stream of revenues. 91 percent of the active and provisional staff and 92 percent of the 'key staff' are board certified. With regrad to increasing managed care in the area, this would be an advantage and could lead to being chosen as provider by managed care plans.

6.3 The Strategic Plan – The Consultants' Conclusions

How should MGH strategically respect all these factors? How did objectives for action plans look like that corresponded with these factors, using the positive outcomes and forces and minimizing or preventing negative impacts?
Below the conclusions and the advice of the professional consultants, are pointed out. Later, it will be interesting to look at business activities that were actually performed by MGH and how their overall direction may differ from the advised plans. Several market trends for the U.P. were determined by the consultants:

- Inpatient procedures were not supposed to increase despite slight population growth and the proliferation of hospital services over the last years, because these inpatient services have already been stable on an average low level over longer time. As a consequence the oversupply of beds could have made it difficult especially for smaller hospitals to work profitable and therefore the importance of collaboration and high quality standards of care is increasing.
- Outpatient procedures were supposed to have an continuing rapid increase, given sufficient facilities. This corresponds with the assumption about growing managed-care and according cost-containment efforts.
- Physician office visits and the need for primary care were expected to increase based on the assumption, that emerging managed care in the U.P would lead to increased use of primary care services versa (more costly) specialty services. To compete, all other payers would continue to tighten reimbursement, too.
- As a conclusions of all research outcomes the consultants finally stated that "in the year 2000, the successful hospital will emphasize and demonstrate operational efficiency, clinical effectiveness, a quality image in the community, a broad base of physician support, financial flexibility, a continuum of services, and collaborative alliances with other providers."

These found trends were transformed into initiatives addressing seven issues setting the direction for MGH's strategic management from 1996 to 1999:

1. Managed care impact on historical hospital utilization, including medical specialist utilization;
2. Hospital's potential new role in financing of health care delivery;
3. Community health needs and the hospital's role in addressing them;
4. Operational improvements in response to the discounts that managed care companies would demand [for their subscribers];
5. Provider network development for the Upper Peninsula;
6. Physician-hospital integration vehicles;
7. Employer/payer perceptions of MGH, its pricing, and its ability to manage inpatients for efficiency and effectiveness.

The consultants' clues for future strategy formulation and goals of management were to take a leadership position in directing and shaping managed care in the Upper Peninsula and pursue collaborative efforts in the development of a regional integrated delivery system.
In accordance with this, MGH also should strengthen alignment with physicians and respond to their needs as a partner in health care delivery or expand selected programs and services. MGH should pay attention to activities which maintain "long-term financial viability while providing superior services and value.

Later in the book, the observation of the actual transformation and integration of this theoretic strategic plan into management decisions will bring to light in what way the professional plan by consultants really targeted MGH, and if it was useful or not. Before doing this, however, the concrete objectives of the advised plan, an extract of the underlying action plans and strategies, have to be pointed out.

Leadership Role and Managed Care: The establishment of a for-profit insurance product in conjunction with the Upper Peninsula Health Care Network is recommended, and furthermore the development of risk sharing products (fee-arrangements with insurance plans and affiliated physicians) under the leadership of MGH. Ownership of a insurance/managed care plan would provide

MGH with additional revenues in a time where the stream of revenues is decreasing.
Doing that in cooperation with other providers would strengthen their interest in not using any other hospital elsewhere but the affiliated MGH as the tertiary provider in the future. Payer-interests and provider-interests provided in one entity represent a chance to measure, improve and control quality more effectively and to keep competitive.

Alignment with Physicians as Partners: The relationship between MGH and the medical community should be enforced by collaborating with physicians and offering expanded management services to physicians in order to excel in a managed care environment. This will in the first place satisfy the needs physicians have expressed in interviews with the consultants.
Furthermore, it would provide the hospital with the opportunity to shape the managed care environment by preparing itself and partners to manage care 'effectively'. Besides, these physician relations would encourage the physicians to give more input into overall management decisions regarding the delivery of care. At last emerging managed care would emphasize the position of primary care and key physicians ensuring the stream of revenue to MGH through referrals. Thus MGH should take care of having sufficient key physicians. This was also important in the light of assuring that also the outlying Upper Peninsula community felt that MGH assisted them regarding the issue 'access to care' and further needs of health care.

Alliance and Network Development: It would be appropriate to strengthen the Upper Peninsula Health Care Network increasingly. The intention was to make other providers use MGH as referral center for tertiary care services. Therefore, the importance of patient care on the local level had to be emphasized by providing primary service with coverage for the entire Upper Peninsula. Rationales were to make other providers refer patients not any longer to out of U.P. facilities for tertiary care.
To overcome the kind of adversarial relationship between MGH and U.P. hospitals, which was seen to cause the loss of patients in tertiary care, collaborative

efforts with other rural providers should substitute former competitive behavior.[a] Such networking and cooperation would lead to a more effective use of resources, contained costs, increased access to care and generally improved health care delivery in the rural communities.

Operational Effectiveness: MGH should develop an integrated clinical and financial information system meeting the information needs of MGH, physicians and affiliated providers. Furthermore, MGH should start an operational improvement program and a labor performance outcome measurement system. This will become necessary because of emerging managed care and the need to "demonstrate value" to become a contract partner of a managed care organization. Apart from this, access to information on all levels and for all providers and customers regarding programs and the effectiveness of an institution was supposed to improve patients satisfaction. At last monitoring and improvement of operational effectiveness would MGH remain profitable under managed care pricing. These prices, utilization and reimbursement for services was supposed to drop in a managed care environment. So it should be MGH's task to answer those tendencies by designing instruments for the quantification and evaluation etc. of resource usage to keep the business effective and profitable.[2]

Reflecting the strategic plan of 1996, the assumptions and suggestions of 1996 in short read as follows: emerging managed care was supposed to play a central role in affecting MGH's further business. Looking at the main key players, former competing providers and the physicians have to be seen as decisive for MGH's position as the tertiary care provider of the Upper Peninsula. Vehicles to reach these goals would be increased networking to increase efficiency and gaining more key physicians as referrers, for example.

This strategic plan represented a combination strategy, including mainly a stability strategy (to keep the status of financial health in a future stamped by managed care), but also retrenchment strategy (to restructure facility and program

[a] Therefore certain programs representing more a collaborative rather than a competitive approach could play an important role and need to be expanded, e.g. Telehealth/Telemedicine.

utilization through collaborative efforts) and a growth strategy regarding recapturing lost percentages in the tertiary care market.
At this point these above mentioned examples shall give some provisional clues for the later discussion. The final conclusions won't be made before having described the actual strategic management process up to 1999/2000 and the factors that shaped it. This – the phase of strategy implementation – shall be subject of the following part of the thesis.
Therefore, chapter seven will point out what the Chief Executive Officer, the Chief Finance Officer and one Board Member thought when they were asked to do a SWOT-Analysis regarding MGH between 1995 and 1999.
It is interesting to see, wether what they said, is in line with the strengths, weaknesses, opportunities and threats as viewed by the consultants in 1995, which were described in the last chapter.
Chapter 8 will then deepen this overview giving detailed information on areas which were seen as important transformation of strategic thinking at MGH in the eyes of the other four Assistant administrators. Both together – the SWOT-Analysis and the examples for strategy transformations into actions plans – then provide a good basis to judge, which overall strategy MGH/MGHS actually took up to 1999, how it differed from the strategic advice of the professional consultants and how certain management processes are rated at the management level. That step will complete the report of all collected and provides the basis on which the study's final conclusions will be made.

---

[1] See Moody's State Health Care Review (August 1995). *Michigan, Marquette General Hospital.*

[2] Tribrook Inc. (January 1996). *Strategic Plan 1996 Marquette General Hospital.* Page 48, see also entire plan. Direct and indirect quotes of the foregone paragraphs refer to that citation.

7 Strengths, Weaknesses, Opportunities and Threats

The following is an abstract of what the Chief Executive Officer (CEO), the Chief Finance Officer (CFO) and one member of the Board of Trustees, the Executive Committee, expressed when asked to name and rate strengths, weaknesses, opportunities and threats of MGH with regard to the strategic plan of 1996 and practice between 1995 and 1999.

7.1 The CEO's Perspective

There are many strengths, some of them lie in the large amount of services MGH provides. Others can be found in a medical staff that has the opportunity to grow, because of an already existing good base and infrastructure of trained personnel that is hard to replace. This hospital has a long history, "it has been in position for 140 years and so there is a tremendous amount of name recognition and sociation to MGH of excellent care." Summarizing the strengths that MGH has, there are: "MGH's people, MGH's technology, and the lot of kind of services that MGH has."

However, there were also weaknesses that existed before or developed within the last years. Points MGH still will have to work on in the future.

> "In many respects the weaknesses that MGH has evolved around the aspect that the population in the area is not growing. In order to grow itself, MGH needs to cure back migration rather than just go higher percentage patients within the population base. A lot of places have an opportunity to expand because of the population expect, but MGH does not have that and has to look at things differently. Because of that, MGH has to look at more expensive outreach physicians to travel."

A lot of money has to be spend to overcome the great distances in the Upper Peninsula, letting physicians travel to destinations as Sault Ste. Marie, Escanaba, Iron River and Iron Mountain.

A last example of a certain weakness, as mentioned by the CEO, is the tightness of space anytime MGH needs to expand. MGH is located in a residential neighborhood of Marquette. That makes it "very expensive to expand for just simple things such as parking or expensive things such as emergency room services."

Nevertheless, MGH's opportunities are still excellent. One rationale is "the overall market share of 27 percent and that could be 100 percent in a lot of areas, but yet [MGH] provides single service for a lot individual things, so in the area of cardiac services, in the area of oncology, in the area of neurosurgery, in the area of physical rehab, in neonatology and so forth. There MGH has the opportunity to increase the market share and expand part of the services." Another type of opportunity is the strong developed information system technology group at MGH. This is needed "to be in position to take advantage of the Internet and electronic means of taking care of and accessing patients."

A threat for MGH is the high competition in health care service. It is not a new threat, nevertheless, nowadays it tends to be more intense.

> "Many places looked in the Upper Peninsula for their patients since MGH looked for their patients. So there is competition and that is becoming more aggressive. Besides there is the threat of decreasing reimbursement from federal and state programs, the changes in the Medicare program affect MGH greatly in business."

Another threat seen by the CEO is that "there is a high shortage, a strain staff right now, that seems to be affecting pharmacists and registered nurses, some other high-tech physicians." Those are the things which always rotate through MGH and affect the business strategy.[1]

This general overview about factors influencing strategic management at MGH is now carried on presenting the view of the Chief Finance Officer.

7.2 The CFO's Perspective

Going through all decisive factors, the good network of hospitals and physicians that work with MGH throughout the Upper Peninsula has to be considered a strength.
There is the cooperative network of clinics owned and physicians employed by MGH which was rated as being excellent. "MGH has a good reputation in terms of Marquette General – the name – in terms of quality."
This strengths correspond with another strength, a good financial health and a good potential with regard to its market share."MGH has a steady growing business and the market is not saturated. A lot of people are leaving the Upper Peninsula and looking elsewhere for health care." And there are potentials with regard to the insurance industry:
First, it is a strength for MGH that it has the status of having its service provision insurance wide covered, which means that all companies respect the designed cost-structure and quality.
Second, the managed care density is still relatively weak, which is a strength, because nationwide managed care has the tendency to depress the charge level and reimbursement, which would negatively impact the financial basis.
And third, as stated by the CFO, "MGH has an interest by insurance companies and others in its business that would like to get its business. That doing good in terms of business with its potentials for growth means also that MGH does not have the fear of layoffs." Furthermore, MGH has a high moral employee force:

> "MGH has the respect of all the people, that they work with, in terms of being fair. The employees are trusting the administration enough, that they know, the administration does everything possible to secure their jobs and pay them well. MGH has done a lot of good human resource programs to ensure the employees, that MGH is a good employer."

In the eyes of the finance officer the sparse land in which MGH is located is also a big weakness. The small number of patients, the great distances to reach patients and facilities and the problem of getting trained and specialized people up to the Upper Peninsula and recruiting them. "MGH has to sell, how good it is living in that rural and distanced area. Another weakness is, like of most health care providers, that MGH would like to get more reimbursement for its services.

> "The government underpays us and the insurance companies underpay us for a lot of services." It is seen as wishful, if MGH could get paid for everything they provide, "because there is needed services out there, but MGH cannot simply afford giving everything to everybody."

From the perspective of the finance officer a good opportunity of MGH is any opportunity that contributes, ensures or improves the status of financial health. One vehicle to keep the status of good financial health and to get increasing independence from the insufficiently paying governments and insurance companies, is the development of an MGH owned insurance plan for the Upper Peninsula. That was the advise also given by the professional consultants in the 1996 Strategic Plan. This advice was transformed into reality with the start up of the 'U.P. Health Plan', which is set up as "a joint enterprise between physicians, hospitals, employers and third party administrators in healthcare development of the Upper Peninsula." The U.P. health plan will not be a provider of health care. In 1999 it was still in the start up phase with the vision of including more and other providers besides MGH.[2]

> "The U.P. Health Plan, which MGH is a major investor in, and has a lot of input into it, is designed to keep health care local in the Upper Peninsula by using health care providers in the Upper Peninsula. It is also designed, so that, what it charges to patient businesses is reasonable and with low costs, so that people will use that insurance product and hopefully the Plan, respectively MGH as owner, provides those customers and businesses with a wide gamut of health care providers here. We can almost do all the services someone needs for health care in the U.P. within the network of providers that are up here including Marquette General. So MGH got away with it to do it all on themselves. MGH just need to coordinate it sale it to the businesses, that is what the U.P. Health Plan is all about. That way MGH cuts out the middleman costs of large insurance companies. The money stays within the U.P. to be used within the Upper Peninsula. That is an opportunity to continue to use it as the managed care vehicle of MGH. It is a vehicle by which cooperation from the other health care providers is gained. It is also a vehicle MGH can use for pricing the products

> and then they turn it around and price it as a insurance product and pass through any discounts that MGH gives to it in order to capture that business. MGH has input in terms of the quality management and utilization review that can go on there, in terms of protocols ... that physicians use in the treatment of diseases and illnesses. MGH has an ability to provide input in that, so that an insurance company does not come along and say: 'We are going to pay only for one day of an OB-stay[a].' With MGH owning of a good chunk of the U.P. Health Plan and the physician input into it, MGH know that such silly managed care initiatives like 'One-day-stays' would not happen.
> The opportunity there is also to find this potential ..., there is a lot of potential, there is a lot of people leaving the U.P., there is a lot of businesses that still hard up on the advantages of managed care as [MGH] sees it, and they can buy into it."

Another advantage for the U.P. Health Plan is that there are no other competitors in this field of managed care within the U.P. except of Blue Cross/Blue Shield. However, they don't have active HMO like the kind of the U.P. Health Plan. And HMOs are generally popular managed care models in the Upper Peninsula thinks the CFO.

> "A [further] opportunity now would be the U.P. Health Plan work with Blue Cross/Blue Shield and jointly offer an HMO in the U.P., so that MGH could offer that attractive product to customers and businesses. And at the same time, MGH would be able to have input into it, so that it is not detrimental to MGH, and that would go in line with the vision of the U.P. Health Plan."[3]

Apart from the CEO and the CFO, there is another authority within MGH's administrative level who can also give a good insight into strengths, weaknesses, opportunities and threats regarding MGH: The Board of Trustees.

[a] 'OB' stands for 'obstetrics'

7.3 A Board Member's Perspective

> "A strength of MGH is where MGH is right now. MGH obviously and for many years had an excellent management right from the top: The momentary CEO had already been in place for twenty-some years as a management person, sitting in many capacities, enabled to come on board and listen and share his expertise with the board. He was a project manager before and he knew where we needed to go. A strength that we have is right with this CEO and the management team and with the Board."

Furthermore, the medical staff and other employees are a strengths of MGH in the sense of needing such a employee base to follow the mission and the vision of MGH. There are the many clinics established within the Upper Peninsula. Besides this facility factor, the Board's member mentions that

> „health care service also depends on the attitude of MGH's fine physicians who take time from their practice, their offices and their families to go on the road with their expertise to treat a person in Grand Marais or Sault Ste. Marie/Michigan or Ironwood for example. They treat those people, who cannot conveniently get to MGH."

Apart from that willingness to travel far distances to take care or the health care needs of U.P. residents far away from the central facility to the clinics, MGH also has the strength of having a commitment to its vision and mission. And the Board's member adds:

> "Marquette General Hospital has a continuous basis, has a vision to know, that the goal is to provide advanced medical service ... for the patients coming through the doors. And there is no discrimination, there is no indication, that, if someone has no proper insurance, that he won't going to be served. MGH not only serves you, MGH takes care of you. MGH has been fortunate to have good financial growth, good management skills and a team of employees from the maintenance people who keep the equipment running to the stores, folks who make sure that all things are in and at the place they need to be, so when a physician or the nurses need something, it is available to the secretaries that we have and not to forget the people in accounting. Without a good accounting background and

> working fine there, MGH wouldn't be able to provide the services, that we provide."

Having a cooperative or committed employee basis and more than 200 specialty physicians can already be seen as a strength. However, being located in a rural setting like the Upper Peninsula might make it hard to attract this medical personnel to work for MGH. But that is not the case, because another strength of MGH comes into play at this point: It is the quality of life and the opportunity to raise one's family in comfortable setting in and around the City of Marquette.

The possible lack of population growth is seen as a weakness also by the Board's member. A lack in patients results in a lack in income for the hospital.

> "[This income is needed] to continue at release updating the services. The other area of weakness was the ability for the hospital and the physicians to work in a cohesive manner together, because there have been tremendous changes in the ability for the physicians and the hospital management and board to work together, so MGH possible weaknesses are becoming strengths."

The tight space of the ground where MGH is built on in the City of Marquette is also seen as a weakness by the Board's member.

> "It is a residential neighborhood. The building of the campus should have been built out in the country, where there is more space rather than in a neighborhood. Now MGH has to do the best they can, not necessarily ever looking to put the residents home into the hospital campus. Many people have sold their homes to MGH." And for MGH it remains to be seen what else they could do. "Maybe 25 years ago, before they did the first expansion, maybe they should looked going elsewhere to do the building. It was never viewed, that MGH would grow into a health system operation, that is so successful.
>
> In terms of opportunities, the example of a recent flu epidemic can function: There is the simple fact that people get sick. And we will be able to take care of them. And the best opportunity is, that we are here and enable them to go home now. The emergency room staff has been overrun with this recent flue epidemic. But that will go away, that will be replaced with people with more serious types of illnesses, that can be handled and saturated. There are the heart patients coming in and the head injury patients, terrible things."

Further, MGH with its clinics and traveling specialists is able to take care of all health care needs locally. Compared with far distanced competitors like Mayo Clinic in Minnesota, most of the patients save money by not having to travel so far and by having family members not staying overnight until the respective medical procedures are completed.

A supposed threat might be that some outside medical service will come in. For example, the cancer treatment program being one of the bests of MGH could be financially hurt through a competitor coming into the service area and providing a cancer program of his own. However, it is the opinion of the Board's member that one should try not to defeat competitors in the sense of: "They are doing good things, we are doing good things. If possible, why not have solved them together and cooperate to turn that fear of something into optimism."[4]

---

[1] Interview with MGH Chief Executive Officer (January 2000). All direct and indirect quotes of this paragraph refer to that source.

[2] See Upper Peninsula Health Plan (U.P. Health Plan) (1999). *Home Page.*

[3] Interview with MGH Chief Finance Officer (January 2000). All direct and indirect quotes of this paragraph refer to that source.

[4] Interview with Member of MGH Board of Trustees (January 2000). All direct and indirect quotes of this paragraph refer to that source.

8 The Transformation of Strategic Thinking into Practice

This chapter will deal with the administration's perspective onto management at MGHS and how the main direction strategic of management looked like. The topic 'changes in the delivery of health care, increasing regional competition, maintaining an adequate flow of patients and decreasing reimbursement' and major strategic answers like efforts to stabilize financial health through collaboration, higher effectiveness and increased attraction of new customers to gain market share will be filled with substance giving concrete action plans and activities at MGH/MGHS between 1995 and 1999.
Interviews with the administrators reveal the actual management path taken by MGH with regard to the focus of the consulting agency onto increasing capital assets, vertical integration and extension of services, interlocking arrangements, cooperation between hospitals, physicians, insurance plans, promoting staff and services and seeking for political support.
The examples and the quantity of the respective comments regarding the areas of strategic engagement (capitals assets, interlocking arrangements and cooperation etc.), the administrators mentioned, can be taken as the important extract of the entire management process representing the major strategic direction at MGH/MGHS between 1996 and 1999. The more one point was mentioned, the more decisive it is supposed to be. Additional information with regard to patient relations and pastoral care within community relations and marketing completes this view with information about patient needs and community needs. This is to observe the (economical) effects of a service area which is not directly contributing to the margin as for example any medical service.

8.1 Staying on the Cutting Edge of Technology

All above mentioned topics and strategic choices are crucial, especially important for MGHS as the regional medical center was to stay on the cutting edge of technology by increasing the investments. High on the agenda was the print of the capitals assets. That was and is also "what the outline physicians, hospitals

and even patients look towards Marquette General for. MGHS has reestablished a good reputation for staying at the cutting of technology."[1]
This is for example shown in the ranking of the 100 most wired list of a survey compiled by PeopleSoft, Compaq and Deloitte Consulting, where MGHS was cited besides five other Michigan health care providers. MGHS exhibits a commitment to using technology to link with employees, physicians, patients, suppliers, insurers and other health care institutions.[2] Examples are the EKG-network and other kinds of technical applications which are pointed out in the following and were already shortly cited in chapter four.

8.2 Establishing Cooperative Arrangements

Another important thing was the cooperation with other hospitals, physicians and insurance plans. The intention is to receive a seamless health care system using those other facilities in concert with MGH where primary care is taking place in the local community and in case of further need MGH has the resources that help out on that end. Therefore, MGH has to work with communities to make them aware of what MGH offers and has at the same time to work with the individual community to protect their own patient basis because of the level of services they can provide. This is hopefully creating a situation whereby people recognize that somebody first goes to his local provider if something more extensive is needed. The natural progression would be then to MGH to a specialist to have a specialized study done or treatment for some disease.[3]

8.3 Critical Access Hospitals

To go in line with the demands to set up cooperative arrangements, MGH is working closely with the other UPHCN hospitals in establishing cooperative types of arrangements, particularly with smaller hospitals up here that have an opportunity to change their designation and improve their reimbursement by going to critical access hospital operation. There are six of those facilities throughout the Upper Peninsula.[4] The regarding MGH administrator, together with these facility administrators, establishes a letter of intent to work with MGH as a sup-

port hospital to make the other facilities critical access hospitals (CAH). A network agreement was developed to get outlined what they are going to do for each other. Four of six hospitals have completed their applications, two of the six have already received a designation and have been accepted by January 1, 2000: Helen Newberry Joy and Schoolcraft Memorial. Two other of the hospitals are still in process of getting the financial feasibility study done, which is a requirement for critical access designation. And the other two are waiting a state survey to get their designation approved.
Doing this, MGH is interested to have a cooperative arrangement so that it is easy for the outline hospitals and physicians that work out there in the rural areas to refer a patient to MGH. What they established is for the real critical patients whether they be heart patient or trauma patients, a 'one call system', where the outlined physicians makes one call to the MGH facility. He talks to the Emergency Room physician MGH has on duty. So there is no delay to get this critical patient from the outline area to our hospital." This kind of collaboration by building up a critical access hospital network (CAHN) is to keep patients within the Upper Peninsula and keep them from going elsewhere. That is what MGH was after.[5]

Not only does cooperation increase economical advantages for MGH directly in form of a higher referral rate, it is also good for the business, indirectly in the sense of benefiting customer friendliness. One Adminstrator says:

> "The cooperation between hospitals, physicians, the collaborate efforts maintaining and improving the relationship that lent themselves to more user friendliness for utilization of MGH's services what they do best here, the hospital MGH or any of our clinics."[6]

8.4 EKG Network

Another example fitting into the range of cooperative strategy is the set up of a Electrocardiogram network (EKG-network). MGH sees to it that hospitals and physicians in outline areas have EKG equipment out there and they transmit EKGs to MGH for interpretation.[7] The outline partners in health care delivery are equipped with updated and useful technology, and this is done through co-operation which functions in a way that MGH works together with their partners when these outline clinics or physicians do their facilities planning to replace equipment or to design new systems within their departments. It is MGH's goal within that cooperative planning process to take into consideration the physician and the user.

> "MGH looks at these physicians as customers as well as their patients and they participate in making capital decisions, capital replacement decisions or in regards to any kind of systems change, a nursing unit, for example, where MGH is doing some changes in the documentation system. Physicians are the ones who need it and so MGH is going to make sure that they are incorporated, that physicians are in there."[8]

Regarding the change of health service delivery, also addressed in the 1996 strategic plan, is e.g. the change process within the behavioral health sector.

8.5 Behavioral Health Service and Rehabilitation

MGH has a behavioral health program which had always a good referral rate throughout the Upper Peninsula. The problem with that program was that it struggled financially (operating costs were not sufficiently compensated through reimbursement). MGH reacted downsizing that program, decreasing the amount of inpatient services, that were provided, and subsequently the number of outpatient services were increased. Described by the respective Assistant Administrator, the intention was the following:

> "MGH established clinics in the outline areas to handle the outpatient care that was needed out there and was then making the appropriate referral back to us on the inpatient side. So MGH has actually in behavioral health decreased [the] overall operating costs on the inpatient side that are now seen in the improvement of the financial picture there."[9]

Another factor that relates to behavioral health is that MGH has an exempt unit. It is exempt from the Prospective Payment System. Despite being out of the Prospective Payment System, the behavioral health is reimbursed under a 'flat fee'. Formerly, this flat fee was not sufficiently covering all expenditures. However, it has moved upwards enough now. MGH works together with the respective intermediaries in Medicare regarding the amount of money that they pay for a patient in behavioral health.

The power of networking can be used in diverse other fields, too. Having clinics providing the outpatient care in the outline communities and referring persons with need for inpatient care back to MGH, this principle works also in the area of rehabilitation.

Apart from the behavioral health program the rehab program is one of MGH's big programs. There MGH works closely together with the three medical directors that direct the rehab program to decrease the length of stay. One idea is a more stringent admission criteria for patients being admitted to the program. Like with behavioral health this is to answer the tougher rate payment over the years. However, rehab is not out of the Prospective Payment System. Compared with behavioral health, in this case not only the way of service delivery (inpatient to outpatient) but the admission criteria was changed to strategically cope with the decreasing reimbursement. Thus MGH got more 'bang for the buck.'

Besides MGH decreased the number of beds, but not as much as in behavioral health. In the consequence MGH had fewer rehab beds as well with improved tougher reimbursement and a shorter length of stay by working with MGH's physicians. Besides the rehab physicians also traveled. They have clinics in four areas and have to go to Sault Ste. Marie, Escanaba, Houghton and Iron Mountain. Again, the purpose of going there is to see those patients out there in that outline area in their home community and determining which patients would be good candidates to come back to MGH's inpatient unit. MGH worked really closely internally with our physiatrists to accomplish that.[10]

8.6 Brookridge Heights Assisted Living Facility

In 1999, MGH made another step forward proceeding on the path enlarging the service range, which begun in the early 1990s with buying Northern Home Health and also included the development of an own insurance product – the U.P. Health Plan. In 1999, MGH started an assisted living project for elderly people, called "Brookridge Heights" in Marquette. This facility is already far being at capacity as far as being full. MGH still needs more space there.[11]
It took only a few months. However, consultants said, it would take up to fifteen months to have it booked out.[12] This reflects the market opportunity that lays in some new areas of business and provides an answer to the question why MGHS is getting into and enlarging such fields of business. It ensures overall financial health and provides subsidization capital for issues like uncompensated care.

8.7 Quality and Cost Control – Strategic Finance Management

The medical records department is involved in reviewing the quality of service delivery at MGH together with other departments. It is their goal to make sure that everything MGH does is of high quality. The process of checking the records is internally called 'abstracting the records' which means to review the records "to gain statistical data to monitor and look at trends in a way patients are treated and the outcomes of it." And this process is an ongoing process. If the quality is on a high level, it is more important for the hospital to keep it there, to maintain this level of quality. The strategic aspect of that is that MGH need to have and to keep a mechanism in place to monitor and feedback to the physicians and administration, how quality is changing.[13]
The control of costs at the hospital is another factor: MGH monitors the costs of services per procedure that is done at the hospital. This data is then compared to the benchmarks of other hospitals in the industry with regard to the costs to do

the service. This gained information is then fed back to the operating managers at MGH to let them know if all or which services are cost-effective or not.[14]
These are examples for the financial process at MGH which further lead to the next step, the budget making process. In this connection between control on the one and new budgets on the other side the strategically important dimension of quality and cost control can be seen. Without the latter, valid decisions about new investments in one service area as part of the overall business strategy can hardly be made.

8.8 HR Management – Promoting Staff Quality and Satisfaction

> "In human resources (HR), the focus is primarily on the employance and to do anything possible to keep the employees as happy as we can possibly do. That is not always easy because MGH is a high stress environment, dealing with life and death type issues"[15]

One way to help satisfying employees and strengthening their labor force can be seen in MGH's compensation program and its history in the 1990s. In the strategic plan of 1996, nothing was said related to the employees and how MGH is going to deal with employee issues.
The history of the compensation program goes back part to 1990. The central point of the compensation approach before was that a new job was in a certain pay-rate, and the employee received an increase each year. This program tired in 1990 and became replaced with 'Pay for Performance.' Certain standards were established that employees had to meet in order to get to the next step of the job classification. But difficulties with that program occured, so it was taken away.

> "It was on management for one thing, because people meeting those standards, would just automatically go up from one to the next step, receiving payment increases from one to the next step from probably 10 percent to 25 or 30 percent. The management was looking at it seriously getting more and more involved with cost containment, prospective payment systems. Quite honestly: the negative of those interests at that time cost the hospital a lot of money."[16]

When the administration at that time turned this around after 18 months, however, the hospital management still felt that there is a need for some sort of organized systematic approach to compensation. MGH did hire a firm to assist them evaluating all the jobs, pay skills and selling skills. There is still a lot of work to be done with that new program called 'Total Comp.' That program is a valuable pay-program. Part of it the compensation program is 'Result Share.' Result share satisfies the economic interests of the business entities (motivating the employees to work harder to achieve higher margins) and makes the employees recognize the pay out of that program because they participate in the economic gains of MGH through the shared profit made. They see how their individual contribution leads to business success of the whole institution and to more money in their own pockets. On the one hand, this is no real team effort, on the other hand, this cannot be seen as an individual effort.

However, these mentioned activities were not drawn from the strategic plan of 1996 because in that plan no human resource related advice was given. This will be changed changed in the upcoming new strategic plan for 2000 to 2003.

Up to this time, the problem should be turned around and putting the employees as being number one will be the first priority. One reason for this can be seen in a unionization campaign of the hourly workers in summer 1999 which can be interpreted as a kind of dissatisfaction with the field of employee relation at MGH. This campaign failed and didn't not lead to any longer labor conflict. However, a potential strike of a group of workers can endanger MGH's economic success[a] and MGH had to set in force an action plan with that preventing such risk.

[a] The potential economical threats for MGH laying in a strike can be deducted from the unionization campaign/a nurse strike in 1994: A two-month nurses strike in August 1994 temporarily interrupted the favorable utilization and financial performance, contributing to a $756,000 net loss first quarter 1995 as reported in Moody's State Health Care Review Michigan: MGH, August 1995.

> "MGH has to stress the confidence of employees, the issue, that MGH has the right people, the right place and the right jobs. MGH has to stress the customer service aspect of that. And that is what we are going to focus more and more. A lot has already been said on customer service. And the CEO preaches at each time the news to the employees. But there are probably more formal programs as it relates to customer service. There is probably more a kind of ability for managers and employees of evaluation as it relates to customer service. That are some things that have to be done here.
> A lot of HR-actions respond to a crisis type of situation sometimes: We have a plan on place and it never fails until something happens."[17]

A plan with regard to a crisis type of situation is probably the 1999 conduction of an employee opiniency study. The participation was very good.[18]
With this the administration targeted the topic of employee satisfaction, motivation etc. and how those prints can be improved.

The new strategic plan for 2000 to 2003, which is not subject of this study, will also be based on results of this previously mentioned study in human resources. Some of the comments within the last paragraph do reveal things that need to be done, not only action plans that were put into practice. They can perhaps be seen as a strategic lack of the 1996 plan and following years of practical management at MGH especially in the area of human resources. Good working employees are a decisive factor also for customer service in general. Satisfied employees are supposed to play an important role in transmitting the good image of MGH to the patient base.
However, this image is not only transmitted by employees, this positioning of MGH in the mind of customers and political key players is also the goal of a separate community relations and marketing department. Their work and their perspective onto overall strategic management is now pointed after the analysis of human resources.

8.9 Community Relations, Governmental Relations and Marketing

Seeking for political support, making political key players aware of MGH and its problems – that is one of the tasks of community relations at MGH. With regard to financial issues with Medicare on the federal level, Medicaid in the state of Michigan or the HCFA, this political support is making sure that the interest of providing care to the patients under whatever political scenario is maintaining MGH's property of reimbursement. That becomes a very critical issue as well as seeing down on the Balanced Budget Act. In 1997, the enactment of the Balanced Budget Act (B.B.A.) on the federal level resulted in diverse attempts to change the negative outcomes of the B.B.A. for diverse providers.[19]

Those outcomes were spending cuts in diverse fields of medical care delivery[20]. Examples for fixes to the B.B.A. are: "Restoring B.B.A. cuts in indirect medical education; addressing concerns with the prospective payment system; and improving payments for skilled nursing facilities, home health care etc."[21]
On several levels the provider community tried to intervene. On the federal level concrete recommendations for B.B.A restorations were introduced as separate bills to the Congress. How that whole process of intervening and lobbying of the health care industry works, becomes clear taking a deeper look on the formulation, the political forces and people behind that and the introduction of one of these bills:
The Rural Health Care Improvement Act (R.H.C.I.A.). It was introduced to the Congress in March 1999 with the intent to improve access to health care services in rural areas. Rural Areas had felt the impact of the Balanced Budget Act stronger then urban areas. Hospitals in rural areas mostly serve a high number of Medicare patients. This reimbursement was shortened through increased application of managed care principles also in the governmental plans Medicare and Medicaid which again affected the provision of skilled nursing, high quality service for those disproportional share hospitals negatively. The loss in revenues made recruiting and retaining health care providers/medical specialists to serve the needs of the rural residents more difficult.

The R.H.C.I.A. included diverse ways of financial relief for rural hospitals, indirectly related to pressures of the B.B.A. Two examples:
One was the idea of the conversions of recently closed or downsized facilities to critical access hospitals by State designation. Outpatient service delivery should be secured by paying amounts equally to reasonable costs or all-inclusive rates. This would have for example insured keeping patients seeking for outpatient care within the U.P. and would have benefited the economic situation of MGHS clinics and all clinics within the UPHCN.
Another amendment were direct Medicare payments for physician assistants, nurse practitioners, and clinical nurse specialists not in the amount of 85 percent, but also 100 percent as usual for regular physicians "in the case of services furnished in an underserved rural area."[22] This would help to better cover health care needs of rural residents and would maybe attract physicians assistants to rural areas, which otherwise would haven't come and they maybe stay later on providing service after being a licensed physician.
Despite the fact that this legislative attempt failed in the later discussion process in the House of Representatives, this bill failed. Not all representatives supported ideas of paying extra money to rural areas[a], but not all ideas included, failed, for example the establishment of critical access hospitals lead to the development of critical access hospital networks promoted by new state laws.

> "Some proposals [like the critical access hospital iniative] fixed to that [finance problem of rural areas], some are simply figured a dike, they aren't very long lasting but they are a help for a while. But continuing to ensure that certain things are protected, particularly in a rural environment, this is absolutely critical to marketing or governmental relations."[23]

[a] That would have partly meant: 'Robbing Peter to pay Paul'. Urban regions had also underserved areas, ghettos in the larger cities, e.g. where the poor and indigent live, which on the one hand wouldn't have benefited from the Rural Health Care Improvement Act and which on the other hand have (city) governments which would have paid into this program like all regions.

Practically, the concrete actions within community relations and marketing look as follows: They represent the several topics of this chapter, from technology as quality issue, over cooperation, access to care strengthened through effective networks and more user friendliness through local provision of care in the Upper Peninsula. community relations and marketing is responsible for the hospital image and how services are promoted in the region.[24]

Focusing governmental relation, the people in this department need to know what is going on in politics and on the legislative level so far as it relates to MGH and health care delivery. Therefore the contact to the certain key players has to be kept. Congresses, meetings etc. of the MHA etc. have to be visited and personal contacts to the representatives have to be strengthened.

The MHA, for example, manages events like the 'Day at the Capitol.' The last one in 1999 had diverse goals, one was to make hospital administrators aware of their tasks in governmental relation and how to do it. That begins with information, how to write a legislator to receive awareness for the respective health care provider and its problems.

Further, the joining health care representatives receive qualitative and quantitative information that make them pay attention to still existing or new threats and opportunities that come along within the market-based U.S.-health system, like taking care of making sufficient margin to compensate problems which might arise with cost containment efforts in Medicaid reimbursement, covering uncompensated care for the indigent and poor people, preparing for "skyrocketing pharmaceutical costs" etc.[25] One source of information and support for hospital administrators is, for example, HEALTH PAC (Political Action Committee). This alliance is consisting of nearly 2000 Michigan health care providers, building a united voice for health care on the state and federal level (here, together with AHA PAC) to build effective and ongoing working relationships with their elected officials. Through Health PAC, support to state and federal politicians (Houses of Representatives) is made possible by the health care community. Thus HEALTH PAC plays an important role in advocacy, for example, lobbying for political decisions mirroring the need of the local medical communities with issues like Medicare/Medicaid spending cuts, Certificate of Need, tax laws etc.[26] Focusing the relation to physicians is another task besides the extensive area of governmental relations. There, community relations and marketing "creates relationships and reinforces relationships between physicians."[27] Thus it perpetuates and fosters communication and exchange between them. A practical example of this is: when a new doctor comes in a medical community "that brings a new procedure, and is newly trained. Following capabilities are here relative to that doctor from the side of the community relations and marketing department: They need to make sure that the other doctors in the region [then] know, that MGH can do the procedure or has people] with expertise that can handle it, whether there is a new physician that brings a new talent or whether there is a new equipment, that brings the ability to do that. Therefore visits by the community relations department, physician relations representatives heading to the referring physicians out in the Upper Peninsula, keeping in loose by phone etc. are important tools to keep the contact between MGH as the regional referral center and the precondition of that: Physicians aware of MGH in Marquette and willing to refer patients to MGHS facilities.[28]

Awareness promoting activities were not only activities targeting physicians to built up effective referral networks on the precondition of mutual awareness of MGH's role and capacity, but of course, they also directly concern the patient. Examples of that are the publication of news about MGH in the local media (newspaper, television), designing brochures and audio-visual patient information or besides that media based way, being involved in the management of events for the community, for example, awarding excellent high school students once a year.

"Those things are the responsibilities of MGH in terms of protecting the image and keeping the image positive." And MGH/MGHS "has a pretty good image among the consumers," as shown in the latest MGH Awareness Study.[29]

Looking at the special service preference and usage in inpatient and outpatient care by customers within the MGH's service areas, MGH was clearly preferred over Mayo Clinic and Northern Michigan Hospitals, the two largest competitors as for March 1999, for every service line (Cardiac, Mental Health/Addictions, Rehabilitation, Accident/Severe Trauma, Orthopedics, Outpatients Surgery, Obstetrics/Gynaecology, Oncology, Neurology/Neurosurgery, Geriatrics and Pediatrics.)[30] Also in 1995 MGH ranked regarding service preference in most service areas on the first place.[31]

It is important to keep in mind, that not only physicians play a role in deciding, where they refer a patient to. The patients themselves are also supposed to express their own preferences vis-à-vis the physician. And therefore the Community Relations and Marketing department is not only interested in being on good terms with referring physicians, but also in being on good terms with the public opinion regarding MGH.

8.10 Franchise Players of MGH – Physician Recruitment

One special area of activity related to physician relation within the area of community relation and marketing is physician recruitment. This department has to deal with instruments of marketing to attract physicians to work for MGH to provide excellent care to the patients on the one hand and to sell these physicians and their talents as show-pieces for MGH to attract new customers on the other hand. Again, this is an example of the different sides customer services is directed to within community relation and marketing. A picture drawn by one administrator is describing, why this extra field of activity, this engagement in physician recruitment and relation was and is strategically critical for MGH. Pointed out by the respective Assistant Administrator:

> "You have to highlight your stars and when you bring in the very sophisticated, newly trained physician who can bring expertise that is perhaps on the cutting of technology or the cutting edge of treatment modalities, that are available anywhere in the country ... it is no different what people in

the United States in sports call franchise players. People want to see the Chicago Bulls play Basketball because of Michael Jordan, people will go see the Green Bay Packers because of Brett Fauve. They are called franchise players.
You promote them and you essentially help the community to be aware of the caliber of physician that is here and most of the people will identify with that as a center of excellence. 'If they got a guy that can do this, that is on the cutting edge of technology in the whole world, then they certainly got a specialist over there just for my little problem.
And that is a little bit of that high academic centers, that promote themselves as this shining star. That is, why so many go into research, because if people think, that these places are research cancer centers, and have the best research in the country, people might go there for their care thinking: 'If they are doing all that, they sure must be able to treat things'.
It is the same idea. Just of a micro-sense, because MGHS does not have an academic setting."[32]

Physician recruitment or building up a high-tech medical care environment, that are examples representing the administration's management function of promoting MGHS as the shining star.
However, this picture of the 'shining star' has its roots originally in religion and beliefs. And this is also plays a role for MGHS's overall management strategy with the 'parental' hospitals St. Mary's and St. Luke's. St. Mary's was the former Catholic hospital of the City of Marquette. In the following these spiritual aspects and if and how they contribute to overall strategic management at MGH are reported based on an interview with director of pastoral care at MGH.

8.11 Pastoral Care and Hospital Administration

The patients in the hospital are the same people who are members of the congregation in small communities. It is a natural thing that they have a kind of social group or religious group who is cooperating with each other or providing pastoral care in the hospital.[33] That are mostly volunteers from the local churches, like the Lutheran, the Roman-Catholic or the Methodist Church. MGH and other large hospitals make it a special point to have chaplaincy departments. In Marquette, former St. Mary's Hospital being the Roman Catholic-sponsored hospital already had a chaplain on staff showing the importance of this kind of relation to the patient.

When MGH grew over the time, the hospital started an official department of pastoral care in the late 1980s with its own director. There is a good relationship – partly on a volunteer, partly on a hired basis – with chaplains in the town's area. The department is at the moment run by a Catholic chaplain as director, the first director was a Lutheran. Not the religious membership, only the capability had an impact on the decision who was and is managing this department.

The largest church membership of MGH's patients is Roman-Catholic with 25-30 percent, the next largest percentage is 7 to 8 percent. Lutherans are 6 to 7 percent. In the country, who is mainly stamped by Lutheran believes, the Roman Catholic church is the largest single religion on the same national average as the patient's religions at MGH and in the Upper Peninsula.

The pastoral care department is connected to the community relations and marketing department and the director and the other chaplains are responsible to the corresponding Assistant Administrator because that part of the hospital has to do so much with the hospital and the relation to the community. Because almost every patient is connected to those churches. However, the responsibility of the Roman-Catholic and the Lutheran chaplains is to all the patients. That includes particularly patients who are not Roman-Catholic, who are not Protestants, who are not Christians. The chaplains are responsible for them "providing spiritual health, support and some guidance and some reinsurance, sometimes in crises with fear or when someone dies. The chaplains have a staff responsibility to support other people who might not have any religious connection at all or might have a Jewish, Islamic or Native-American spirituality ensuring responsibility for their spiritual well-being and support. Described by one chaplain:

> "Even, when patients or their families are not religious people, they see the chaplains helpful in helping them being in touch with the spiritual part

> of their life, their sense of god and religion, spirituality and mortality, their own death, and the fear related to that."[34]

Having such a department, also pays off on another level which highlights the need for chaplaincy work at a hospital and so at MGH:

> "Patient survival, patient recovery has lot to do with their sense of hope and with their sense of spiritual support that is measurable, that is medically and scientifically measurable."[35]

MGH is providing access to health care services to improve the health status of residents of Marquette County in the Upper Peninsula and the surrounding region. Part of improving that health status of the people is their spiritual health, not just because it is nice, but spiritual life relates directly to physical and psychological health. Medical and psychological studies are rediscovering that people who pray or go to churches are medically healthier than those who do not. Thus among other things, the hospital provides chaplain's care to make people physically healthier. This also reflected in another quote of one chaplain:

> The insurance industry has discovered, that hospitals that have a chaplain's department get sued less often because the patients and the families have a sense: somebody cares about me, somebody prays with so and so that is dying. So from the strictly material point of view, the hospital saves a lot of money, having a chaplain on the staff."[36]

How about patient relations in a broader sense besides spiritual needs? That is the area of responsibility of the patient advocate. Which tasks, which opportunities are there to find, that include strategic factors, like promoting patient satisfaction that are important to be recognized designing an overall strategy for MGH?

8.12 The Patient Advocate and Customer Service

The patient advocate is involved with customer service, the individual concerns of patients and their families, but, more in a practical sense if compared with the work of a hospital chaplain. The task of the patient advocate is to work with patients, physicians, nurses and the administration to solve problems like concerns or complaints of patients feeling unsatisfied with any service they have received at MGH. Examples of patients' complaints are billing issues, the way of care and service is delivered, 'lost and found' issues and the personal atmosphere at the hospital.[37]

"A typical complaint is about billing, where the work of patient advocate in co-operation with the billing office begins at the point when a patient has the feeling that she or he paid for some procedure he or she never received. Therefore, MGH set up the rule that everyone is alert to have an itemized statement. That means, that everyone can get a statement from the business office that itemizes all the treasure. Sometimes, the people also complain about having to have that statement. If people go through and feel, that they didn't receive any thing or treatment, the hospital is forced to make adjustments regarding the itemized statement or to discuss the problem with the patients to make them understand the sense behind that statement and the hospitals behavior. Those adjustments have to be seen more as arrangements for the insurance companies to ensure coverage. Sometimes they are misunderstood by the patients as measures primarily for themselves, but it is more for the insurance and that the hospital "is kind of out of the chart."
Other complaints that have to be solved to directly satisfy the patient, are:

> "Complaints about the care the patients received and of course about nurses and physicians. One thing the hospital and the patient advocate is tracking are patients coming in for procedures at 5 o'clock in the morning and not being down until noon or afterwards. And they are pretty unhappy about it. So the patient advocate is trying to find out where the problem started. The ban of [the patient advocate's] life, however, are lost glasses, walkers, prosthetic things etc."

So in every situation and regarding every kind of complaint it is the patient advocate's job to function as the roaming trouble-shooter recognizing concerns and difficulties in the hospital's all-day-life and then trying to turn these things around, improving the customer service and so the whole atmosphere between all people meeting in the hospital.
The starting point for the position of the patient advocate at MGH evolved in the 1980s with a legislative change in the Medicare reimbursement effecting the numbers of patients. It was the hospital's plan, to keep in touch with all the patients and get to know, what they like about the place" and how it could be improved. patient relation has become an issue of growing importance in that time, because people are much more aware of that 'right' founded in the legislation so far as health care and they have many more questions with regard to legislation, reimbursement etc. than they have been twenty or fifty years ago.
To improve the atmosphere, talking to patients is not the only factor, reacting to employee memos regarding any complaining patient, and making unsolicited visits in departments is also necessary. The feedback, the individual opinion of physicians and nurses is also crucial. Therefore the prior acceptance of the patients' advocate's work is a prerequisite. Nobody would listen to the patient advocate and change his or her behavior if that job position was not respected by the staff. Two points are key factors for earning this respect:
One is the independence of the patient advocate at MGH with regard to higher levels of management, the other thing is the way how to approach physicians and nurses with complaints of their patients if they are involved or subject of the complaint.
The Patient Advocate does have a lot of independence. Even this position is subordinated to the according assistant administrator, the patient advocate is careful not to talk to anyone else about a problem. It is requested to build up trust and from the point of responsibility to any higher authority the patient advocate is allowed to do that. Through that independence, people come to the patient advocate not only for small-talk, they come "just to really invent" if there is complaint about any patient on their floor or if they heard, that there is some complaint about a nurse or so. Then it is on the patient advocate to calm down

the emotions by first to talking to the corresponding employee, and second, if it is needed building up a connection to the right authority. The patient advocate introduces, for example, the according supervisor of that employee or helps to refer the person to the Assistant Administrator of human resources, if there are complaints about the way somebody was treated by a nurse or so. However, it depends on what the concern is. Sometimes family conferences are a promising vehicle to solve a problem. For example, relatives are wondering, why procedures or stays take longer then expected. They have maybe problems to stay informed about the proceedings and the treatment of their relative because the family members are widespread throughout the entire Upper Peninsula or neighboring states having to cope with the isolated location of MGH. In such case and if any problem arose, family conferences would be set up by the patient advocate to bring together all family members and the people who are working with the patient and the relatives, like therapists, physicians, nurses etc.

The primary job of the patient advocate so is to function as a gateway for worried, concerned customers and staff members.

The other function of being respected is the resolute behavior and the steady contact with physicians and nurses. In the first time the patient advocate still had to fight with a lack of trust or respect. Many first thought, that today's patient advocate "was against the law. They were suspicious about people," however, that first mistrust was overcome by getting to know each physician, having meetings, being in a kind of steady and good contact with everyone. This sometimes loose way of communicating with doctors enabled the patient advocate also to discuss the critical things, the complaints.

Families are for example entitled to know what is going on with their relative in the hospital an the doctor need to be telling them. Then the earned trust and respect is a good basis also to confront a doctor with a more direct complaint in the way of critically saying: "You know, the family is really upset and we need to have a meeting," which doesn't mean, that there are always concerns about physicians or their way of talking to patients. "Some of them are very good of immediately going to talk to a family" and solving problems by themselves, but "some aren't very good in interacting" However, still "a lot of them are reluctant to react and solve the problem."[38]

Summarizing these examples, one can say: If there is a problem of not understanding maybe complicated reimbursement policies or if it is one of the reluctant exemptions within the staff group not answering the patients concerns, there is this need of an mediator position. And that was answered by the hospital to install and keep the position of the Patient Advocate besides general support and practical help done by social workers and the spiritual service of the pastoral care department.

8.13 The Strategic Basis – Networks, Teams and Symbiotic Partnerships

When reviewing all areas of activity within Marquette General Hospital, the mentioned examples within the several departments fit under the umbrella of net- and team working. Networking was done on the institutional level, beginning already with the facility expansion plans, and buying clinics in the early nineties, which proceeded with developing ideas for a institutional frame for all of that which was at the end Marquette General Hospital converting into Marquette General Health System.

That process was accompanied by diverse strategic networking efforts as shown in foregone interviews made about the late management history of MGH. To complete and summarize all proceedings with the special focus on networking, plans to set up the U.P. Health Care Network started already in the mid-1990s.
This collaborative idea became a provider network, now comprising of MGH as regional medical center, 13 community hospitals, a Medicaid management plan and later the realization of legislative options to secure ongoing health care delivery also in rural areas, designing the critical access hospital network rescuing clinics within the UPHCN from being downsized or closed.
Further sponsored cooperative arrangements within the UPHCN are the Upper Peninsula Poison Crisis Network and the Hospital Home Care Network, joint purchasing of health care/pharmaceutical goods, a network of primary care and specialty physician outreach clinics with MGH as the referral center.

Finally important are also a network of cardiac services, stress testing, the U.P. Medical Library Consortium, the U.P. Teleradiology and Teleconferencing Network, a reference lab network, and the U.P. Regional Blood Center. Further the UPHCN is starting a U.P.-wide integrated information system network connecting the diverse hospitals and streamlining patient care delivery.[39]
Several grant programs support those tendencies of streamlining and improving health care in rural areas.[40]

However, optimizing the efficiency of patient care, that is and was also the goal of another strategic management effort on the social level, as shown in the area of patient relation, human resources or physician relation and governmental relation: Team-working. The letters in ‘team’ already express the goal:
T-ogether e-veryone a-chieves m-ore.

Of course, both expressions ‘networking’ and ‘teamworking’ are interchangeable or substitutable by expressions like symbiosis. That is for example the case with the planned ownership structure of the U.P. Health Plan where the hospital provider side with the Hospital Network LLC and the physician side with the U.P. Physician LLC set up a 50/50 partnership to sell the insurance product.[41] The physicians are interested in patients to treat, the hospital providers to keep their institutions running by renting practice space to physicians or to get referrals for specialty hospital treatment by physicians out in the country. Both interests finally depend on available money which is provided by insurance.

8.14 Virtual Networking and Teamworking via Telehealth

For a few years now there has been the Upper Peninsula Telemedicine Network additionally to the clinic and hospital network existing. This network connects health care facilities in the U.P. via local and wide area networks. In the beginning, the network was originally deployed to offer continuing medical education to rural healthcare providers. In that capacity the network has expedited training, kept medical staff informed of new procedures and products, and eliminated the expense and lost productivity of travel. Following the system’s installation,

MGH's affiliates quickly discovered its telemedicine and administrative potential. Today, special IT-systems support a broad base range of health care applications, including psychiatric consultations, surgical follow-ups, tumor conferences, and patient staffing (post-release meetings with patients and local caregivers).[42] Also with regard to the newly set up Upper Peninsula Critical Access Hospital Network, this technical support via telemedicine applications is planned to be used in emergent and non-emergent care, providing electronic based physician consultation through MGHS to maximize a seamless delivery of care.[43]

A further chance within the use of such technology is the vision that it can link health care providers especially those in rural far distanced areas to state and federal institutions, so directly and in an efficient way connecting for example community hospitals with the grant giving institutions in Lansing or Washington D.C. or where ever like the Health Care Financing Administration Health Resources and Services Administration etc.[44]

---

[1] Interview MGHS-SMAUSHC-1.

[2] American Hospital Association (February 1999). *Health Care's 100 Most Wired.*

[3] See interview MGHS-SMAUSHC-2.

[4] See interview MGHS-SMAUSHC-1. The following paragraph is based on this reference.

[5] Closing citation interview MGHS-SMAUSHC-1.

[6] Interview MGHS-SMAUSHC-2.

[7] See interview MGHS-SMAUSHC-3. The following paragraph is based on this reference.

[8] Direct quote and closing citation for indirect quotes: Interview MGHS-SMAUSHC-3.

[9] Interview MGHS-SMAUSHC1. The following entire paragraph is also based on this citation.

[10] Closing citation interview MGHS-SMAUSHC-1.

[11] Interview MGHS-SMAUSHC-4.

[12] See Interview MGHS-SMAUSHC-1.

[13] Interview MGHS-SMAUSHC-9. The following entire paragraph is based on this citation.

[14] Closing citation. See Interview MGHS-SMAUSHC-9.

[15] Interview MGHS-SMAUSHC-5. The following entire paragraph is based on this citation.

[16] Interview MGHS-SMAUSHC-5.

[17] Interview MGHS-SMAUSHC-5.

[18] Closing citation. See Interview MGHS-SMAUSHC-5.

[19] See Interview MGHS-SMAUSHC-2.

[20] See U.S. Congress (1997). *Balanced Budget Act of 1997,* and: American Public Health Association (1999). Balanced Budget Act of 1997 Fact Sheet.

[21] American Hospital Association and American Association of Medical Colleges (April 1st 1999). *Letter to affiliates.* Page 2.

[22] U.S. Representative Nussle (March 16th 1999). *Discussion Draft, A bill to promote and improve access to health services in rural areas.* All indirect quotes in this paragraph also refer to that source.

[23] Interview MGHS-SMAUSHC-2.

[24] See Interview MGHS-SMAUSHC-2.

[25] Johnson, S. (1999). *Key Messages – 1999 Day at the Capitol.*

[26] Michigan Health and Hospital Association (February/March 1999). *Health PAC News.*

[27] Interview MGHS-SMAUSHC-2. The entire following paragraph is based on this source

[28] Closing citation interview MGHS-SMAUSHC-2.

[29] Interview MGHS-SMAUSHC-2.

[30] See MWM Marketing Research and Consulting (1999). *1999 Awareness Study MGH: Hospital Service Area Awareness and Attitudes - Topline findings.* Page 2.

[31] See Matousek and Associates (1995*). Awareness Study MGH Findings.*

[32] See Interview MGHS-SMAUSHC-2.

[33] Interview MGHS-SMAUSHC-6 The entire following part up to the next citation is based on this interview.

[34] Interview MGHS-SMAUSHC-6.

[35] Interview MGHS-SMAUSHC-6.

[36] Closing citation. Interview MGHS-SMAUSHC-6.

[37] See Interview MGHS-SMAUSHC-7. The entire following part up to the next citation is based on this interview.

[38] Closing citation Interview MGHS-SMAUSHC-7.

[39] See Upper Peninsula (1999). Health Care Network *Services – Overview* (Web Site).

[40] See Office of Rural Health Policy (February 1999). *Rural Hospitals, Clinics, and Networks; Rural Hospital Flexibility Program; Rural Health Outreach* and … *Grant Program.*

[41] Upper Peninsula Health Plan (U.P. Health Plan) (1999). *Home Page.*

[42] See PictureTel (1996). *Case Study: Training and Education [at MGH].*

[43] Marquette General Health System (1999). *Letter of Intent, Critical Access Hospital Agreement.*

[44] Puskin, D. S. (Office for the Advancement of Telehealth). (Spring 1999) *From the Feds ... OAT: Giving High Tech Ideas the Human Touch.*

9 Strategic Orientation and Staff Opinion

9.1 Non-Profit Management between Margin and Mission

Having drawn a picture of factors forming MGH's strategic decisions up to 1999 and giving selected background information on diverse strategy relevant issues, this chapter will now point out the tense relationship between the factors mission and margin driving non-profit hospitals. The chapter deals with the question which strategy orientation is better for the hospital's administration: to keep the institution running economically favourably and/or in accordance with the community's interests. Where are the advantages of putting the mission high on the business agenda of a non-profit hospital and where are the advantages in the case of putting margin first before other goals?
First, some contributions to this discussions of health care professionals and representatives, scientists or consultants are given.
'No mission, no margin' or 'No margin, no mission'. It will be interesting to look at these mottos in comparison with the previously given information on MGH's history and environment, the management experiences of the last years. What motto stood for MGH?
The third part of this chapter deals with the opinion of the department heads and program directors of MGH. How do they rate certain potential components of an overall strategy within the range between margin and mission goals and with regard to the relation of non-profit management, ethical demands and economical ratio? Again, the question is: Which of both mottos do they think is proper?

9.2 No Margin, No Mission or No Mission, No Markup – What Makes Starbuck's Differ from Most Health Care Providers

It is a point of discussion in the non-profit health care environment if the provider's margin depends on how well they sell their mission as something that is part of the special product or brand of non-profit providers or if the commitment to provide uncompensated health services to poor patients as determined in the mission statements of non-profit hospitals, is depending on a sufficient margin.

To directly effect the margin positively, most people think that increasing service delivery and therefore expansion projects are useful and needed. Without those efforts, the margin won't be effected positively. Margin-oriented measures could be product and service development, increased performance of the employee force, improving productivity and efficiency of the particular work procedures minimizing costly threats like unionization campaigns, and lowering the amount of services and procedures, where no financial compensation (revenue) can be expected for, things that are clear and monetarily measurable.
There are also factors that are might be overlooked and contributing to a positive margin. Things that need to be done because of contracts, legislation or ethical commitment that is not primarily following market-based principles: The provision of uncompensated care which later needs to be cross-subsidized and hospital-internally by using revenues from paying patients or saved money through the tax-exempt status.

The Balanced Budget Act (BBA) brought up this discussion again. Non-profit hospitals asked themselves bearing in mind their general losses through non-market logical uncompensated care how to deal with the BBA's consequences and how to fight back the potential economical pressures.
The Association of American Medical Colleges (AAMC) also thought about that: The Balanced Budget Act forces hospitals to cut back on their mission, but it remains a point of discussion if cutting back the mission does ensure the economical future or might hurt more than it helps.
Balanced Budget Act reductions could force major teaching hospitals to cut community services and care to uninsured, the AAMC warned. To preserve the hospital's mission, one suggestion was to restore indirect medical education (IME) and disproportionate-share payments to pre-BBA levels. The BBA generally was seen as a threat posed to the financial stability, driving down the total margin with potential harmful impacts on hospitals and the community they serve.
The statements of the AAMC representatives are worth being looked at in this thesis, not so much with regard to the situation of teaching hospitals in special, but in the sense of the main conclusions which is that more money is needed to

keep the mission of a hospital to keep the services provided to the community. One example of this is: not having to shut their emergency rooms to new patients, as did other institutions. Margin stabilization comes before the mission, which is supposed to depend on the margin.[1]

That is also the view of the Michigan Hospital Association, despite of the fact, that all Michigan community hospitals, all members of the MHA, are nonprofit entities whose perspective is supposed to be eventually seen not exclusively 'margin'-focused. The MHA published a brochure in 1999 discussing the question, why there is a need for margin first if you are a non-profit provider with a mission to care for health care needs of the entire community. They say regarding the experiences of the last years:

- A non-profit hospital must make a sufficient margin to ensure financial viability and quality of care
- By virtually any yardstick, current margins of Michigan hospitals are insufficient to fulfill their community-based, nonprofit mission.

These arguments are supported by the fact that each of Michigan's non-profit hospitals is governed by a Board of Trustees whose members are from the community the hospital is located. As described, one of its tasks is taking care of where the money flows that is spent by the hospital. Since the non-profit hospitals' status requires not to give money back to any stockholders, the margins earned by these providers are exclusively re-invested in programs and services that meet the health care needs of the community.[2]

In the eyes of the MHA, these programs and services meet the demands of the surrounding community because of the Board members affiliation with that area. That is seen not to be right for for-profit providers where the decision-making authority often resides outside the community or the State and where the money earned is given to a large extend to stockholders or maybe fund operations of other operations outside the respective community.

Additionally to the regular programs and services provided for the community, also certain medical services were sponsored by the MHA (1998 coverage) like:

- Subsidized specialty clinics and services (2,819,000 persons served)
- Primary care clinics for the uninsured (902,000 persons served)
- Health screenings programs (334,000 persons served)
- Community education and outreach (2,412,000 persons served)[3]

Making a sufficient margin ensures the ongoing service provision and the quality of the regular and the charitable services for the community.
There are clear rationales, why especially non-profit hospitals need a positive margin to carry on providing their range of care: On the one hand, they have the same expenditures as for-profit hospitals, but on the other hand, they have not that many options to increase the flow of money besides the regular service reimbursement.
There are certain regular cost drivers not only non-profit hospitals are facing:

- Salaries and benefits to attract and maintain the medical staff and/or satisfy employees;
- Medical technology, procedures and services have to be up to date to attract customers/patients, therefore buildings and medical equipment have to be modernized or replaced.

However, there are only a few ways how non-profit hospitals can earn a sufficient margin to finance these points mentioned above compared with for-profit hospitals:

- Issuing bonds, that means financing capital investment through debts. Gaining money by selling stocks on the equity markets is not allowed for non-profit hospitals.

- Saving profits, if not needed, as reserves for certain projects. This directly emphasizes how important a positive margin is. Only by making a surplus this way of financing capital investment can be taken.[4]
- And at last, money is saved through community property-tax exemptions for non-profit service delivery including uncompensated care etc.[5]

Thus following a margin is substantial even for mission-orientated non-profit hospitals. The ability to follow the mission is causally linked to the availability of money. That sounds logically right. However, there are people, who don't follow this view. Some hospital administrators (as shown in their comments later) and also the worldwide director of health care strategy for Arthur Anderson, a professional consultant, base their opinion on economical ratio and profit orientation rather than on compassion for issues of the uninsured. Those people don't support a motto like 'no margin, no mission'.
Brian Wong, the consultant, comes to the conclusion: "No mission, no markup." The other way following only income orientated strategies and worrying about the margin before other things would "first mark the beginning of a hospital's death spiral." Wong gives an example of a successful business venture to support his motto:

> "When Starbucks took the lowly coffee bean, a commodity, and elevated it to an experience, healthcare has taken the most important human experiences and reduced them to the level of commodity. [However,] bottom-line thinking hurts hospitals' most marketable assets."[6]

Margin orientated managing would lead to decreased customer service, more complaints and the failure of a hospital to make itself attractive by being distinct. The other way, creating awareness of the hospital first, putting the spotlight on the unique brand of the hospital, increasing customer service and employee development first, would later enable the hospital to have a better position for negotiations of improved reimbursement. The earned profit through more customers and more active employees could then be used for construction financing etc.[7]

With regard to this point, it remains questionable if facilities and equipment update, even if it is not directed by the community relations department of a hospital e.g. or by the indirect customer service can be seen as attractive and beneficial to (new) customers.

For hospital management, it will be more important to know and to decide, in how far, mission and margin are parallel goals of an overall strategy. Probably, with the motto 'no margin, no mission', is used simply to cut a long story too short.

In the following paragraph this question will be discussed further and the previously mentioned viewpoints will be completed, breaking down this question to MGH. What does the administration level think, what was the guide-line and motto for MGH's strategy generally and especially between 1996 and 1999? Was it 'no mission, no margin' – or in congruence with the MHA actually 'no margin no mission'?

9.3 The Administration's Perspective on Margin and Mission

Taking into account the opinion of the Chief Executive Officer (CEO) and the five assistant administrators including the Chief Finance Officer (CFO), four people said, 'no margin, no mission' and two decided, that 'no mission, no margin'. Two decided 'no margin, no mission' could be taken as motto for strategic management at MGH process for the foregone years or reflecting their general point of view. As reasons for their perspective to look onto strategic management, the following statements were made with regard to a potential motto for MGH and other non-profit-providers:

9.3.1 No margin, No Mission and its Certain Balance

- "If you don't have a margin, you do not have the mission. You can have all kinds of missions. But if your mission is set, that you won't make any money out of it, you won't stay in business. You need a margin in order to continue the mission that you might have in all the various places that you have."[8]

- "No margin, no mission, because you certainly have to be able to finance your mission. And so you have to pay attention to the margin. That is, where my philosophy is, I always said that administrators worry about the financial aspect, my next level of management worries about force, finance and quality, and when you get to the bottom, they are worrying about the quality and are not thinking about the costs and that is kind of the way you want it because you want the person, the nurse, taking care of the patient focused on quality. And you have the next level worrying about costs and quality making sure it is balanced. And the next is watching the bottom-line. The process of making the mid-management understand, that there has to be a certain balance. Sometimes it is simply impossible to make them understand. The big thing to getting them understand is knowledge, information and communication. You just got to make sure that they have an understanding about what is going on. And they are allowed and able to communicate back, to get feedback and that there is a two-way communication. And that is one of those things, that are just constant, because in health care it just has been not that long ago where money was never an object in health care. If you bought a piece of equipment, it was paid for. Now we have to look at it a whole lot different. We spent a lot of time that we had to go through this change. But it is not always remembered. So we need to constantly communicate."[9]

- "No margin, no mission. In order for us to continue, we have to have the money to do it. And there has to be, even we are a non-profit health care system, excess money available over our expenses first to continue to expand and it is important that all hospitals have the ability to generate an excess over their expenses, so that they can continue to expand and buy some of the new technology available. It is true for small rural hospitals up here as well as us. We see it on a much larger scale because of how big we are and the services we provide and the lot of specialty areas. So you just have to have the money to make it work. It is a bottom-line."[10]

- "No margin, no mission, because the fact of the matter is: If you do not have resources, your intentions may be very good, ... a good example [is] Mercy Health System in Detroit. They lost $139 million in the last two years. They are closing on March 1 [2000]. A hospital 300plus-bed-hospital is closing, shutting down. Okay, my point is: They had a very significant mission. They were known in Detroit as the hospital that cares for the indigent. They had a Medicaid population. They provided good service to people who would otherwise would go without.

That meant: No reimbursement. That mission no longer continues. That hospital was owned by a religious order, which further enhances my story – the mission.
That seems to be more careless and is probably not the company MGH line. But the fact of the matter is, that without a margin, your mission of providing the best care to your patients, recruiting the best doctors, having a good equipment, doing the things that you need to do, especially being a treasury hospital, especially at our level is dramatically changed by the resources that you have available. And if you do not have them, if you are not financially viable, you create a situation, where you have a bit of a chronic degeneration of each program. Once that begins, it begins to unravel. And once a doctor is here and says: All I asked for two years ago was the machine and they got no money. How long do you think, will he stay? He is going to go. You lose that physician, you lose that ability to provide that service and so on. It is a domino effect. If you are recognizing that your margin is not there to support services, you have to alter that mission because you would jeopardize the rest of the organization. As a generic overall statement: The idea is, why would you alter the mission to maintain the margin?"[11]

9.3.2 The Other Perspective: No Mission – No Margin

"Because we are a non-profit institution, the number one thing, we have to do, is to serve our population, we have to do that. We obviously cannot do it without money, but I would think, that mission is more important than margin. The best example for that is to look on it from a macro basis and to look at it on a micro basis: when a patient comes into the Emergency Room seeking treatment, you treat the patient first, than ask for the money. We do not ask for the money and then treat the patient. So it is more important to accomplish our mission than to make a margin. That is the truth of the matter, because that is, what a non-profit institution is all about.
No mission, no margin. The mission establishes the goal, a mission sets up the direction. Without a mission you loose your way a little bit. With a mission, you know the direction, where you want to go, the programs you want to develop. Usually you have your mission supported by your margin. That is extremely important."[12]

9.4 The Administrators' Preferred Strategy

The administrators were asked to prioritize five issues of strategic management, which were the ones that make up the overall business strategy in the strategic plan of 1996. Independently of that plan they represent key areas of activity for MGH, from finance to marketing based on the experiences and talks the author of this study had within his internship.
Also all department heads of MGH were asked to fill out questionnaires dealing with these five issues of strategic management. They were testing the mid- and lower management's opinion with a catalogue of diverse indicator questions trying to find out, in which points and to what extent the opinion within the administration level of MGH is congruent within all levels and how they maybe differ from one another. This data regarding the line of sight at MGH can be later used to evaluate the strategic management process, the way of organization internal communication of the late 1990s.
To prioritize strategic elements for an appropriate overall business strategy for MGH to cope with financial and social concerns and threats, and to use strengths and opportunities the following strategic planning elements were given:

- Increase of capital assets;
- Vertical integration of services and extension of services;
- Interlocking arrangements and
  cooperation between hospitals, physicians, insurance
- Improved quality of existing staff and services;
- Search for political support.

The above mentioned prints and their importance for MGH in general and especially within the late 1990s were prioritized by the administrators as follows (see explanatory examples in chapter seven and eight): First it should be mentioned that a couple of administrators strengthened the point that the diverse ways of coping with decreasing reimbursement, increasing competition or a changing demands for health care delivery etc. are "all equally important"[13] and that except of the cooperation vehicle, "the other options are somewhat unilateral instead of neutrally acceptable"[14]

Nevertheless, most often on the first and second positions, efforts to cooperate with other health care providers in the U.P. were mentioned.

- "The best way of coping with concerns and threats is probably the cooperation between the hospitals, physicians and insurance plans. In healthcare you have to work with everybody, there is not a taking over of somebody and to win a market because you cannot take over everybody. Even if you employ physicians, you still need to work with them, you do not own physicians as employees and you do not own other hospitals or their communities. Even you own the assets of the building or you may employ the people there, it is always more important to gain the cooperation of the people that you are working with."[15]

- "The cooperation is the number one issue. We at MGH have learned since the strategic plan of 1996 to foster positive relationships between the hospitals within the Upper Peninsula, but their relationship with the physicians out in the community as well and certainly with the insurance plans to some degree. In the major theme of the 1996 Plan 'Managed Care' we never came to fruition here in the Upper Peninsula. The collaboration with the physician community, the other providers – insurance plans to some degree (see also chapter seven), is probably the essence of what drives the business."[16]

Secondarily decisive was the quality control and improvement of services and staff. That also includes described quality reviews by 'abstracting the records', specialist recruitment, education and HR activities.

- "The quality issue, the services ... provide the recognition of your quality" and it goes hand in hand with the cooperation.[17]

- "The second issue that has to be focused is the quality of staff and services and the recruitment of specialists because you have to make sure that the product, which is healthcare that you are selling, is a high quality product."[18]

Apart from this, paying attention to quality the 'vertical integration of services' (primary health care service, insurance, nursing care etc.) was rated as thirdly important, for the purpose of gaining efficiencies in the delivery of care.
That issue was less mentioned and emphasized than the above mentioned ones, but put before 'Search -for political support'. Placing those last issues on position three and four of a ranking of elements being appropriate for an overall strategy does not mean that those issues rated as unimportant. Political support for example, was (nevertheless) seen as "extremely important,"[19] too. Only one administrator differed from this ranking much in one point, taking the issue of 'increasing capital assets' as his number one issue of an overall strategy for MGH through first investing in new technology besides other ways of strategically managing the hospital and to strengthen MGH's reputation. The other respondents were not mentioning 'increasing capital assets' at all.

This is a short review, how the upper management of MGH ranked those strategy relevant business components. In the following the opinion of the department heads at MGH with regard to comparable issues is reported. Their opinion was found out via sent out questionnaires containing indicator questions helping to unravel their true believes about the overall direction MGH has taken (or should have taken).

9.5 The Department Heads' and Program Directors' Preferred Strategy

Is there a congruency between the outlook of MGH's strategy with the department head's and program directors' opinion about what?
And to which extent or with regard to which points this can be tested by looking at the results of the questionnaires?
The following issues or variables represent certain concepts of strategic management. In difference to the open interviews with the administrators on which the content the last paragraphs/chapters were based, the following paragraph

consists of the rating results in percent[a]. The department heads and program directors were asked to rate the issues on a nominal five-point-scale. Before the exact rating results are shown in form of tables, the tested theses are mentioned.

9.5.1 Development of New Fields of Business

Broadening the service range in general is important to meet the customers' demands more efficiently.

Adding new services, like health insurance offerings (the U.P. Health Plan), makes MGH less dependent on government based payment plans like Medicare and Medicaid.

However, the broadening of the service range may lead to a lowering of the respective service quality

Table 5 New Fields of Business

Rating of Importance (%)	Very much	Much	Undecided	Not much	Not at all
Broadened Service Range	52.3	40.9	2.3	2.3	2.3
U.P. Health Plan benefits Margin	6.8	34.1	27.3	25.0	6.8
Additional Services, less Quality	--	2.3	6.8	34.1	54.5

[a] Numbers may not add to hundred because of rounding and totally differing or undefined answers.

9.5.2 Investing in New Buildings and Technical Equipment

Customers are more attracted by renovated and new facilities than by any internal show-pieces like excellent services.
Those modernized facilities enable the medical, nursing and administrative staff to perform more efficiently. -
There is a positive effect of a shiny and well-equipped work environment onto the staff motivation.

Table 6 Investing in New Buildings and Technical Equipment

Rating of importance(%)	Very much	Much	Undecided	Not much	Not at all
New facilities versus service show-pieces	--	15.9	18.2	54.5	6.8
Modernization enables work efficiency	55.0	45.5	--	4.5	--
Modernization motivates staff	40.9	50.0	2.3	4.5	2.3

9.5.3 Staff Training, Customer Friendliness and New Ways of Treatment

Friendly and open-minded doctors and nurses make patients feel safe and make them come back, if they need further health service.

More offerings in special medical research and treatment prevents patients from seeking health care at competing health care institutions.

In-house-training for all employees is important to keep abreast of new management strategies, new ways of medical treatment or nursing behavior etc.

Table 7 Staff Training, Customer Friendliness and New Ways of Treatment

Rating of Importance(%)	Very much	Much	Undecided	Not much	Not at all
Friendly staff affects patient affiliation	77.3	22.7	--	--	--
Specialty research / treatment	29.6	47.7	13.6	6.8	2.3
In-house-training to keep abreast	61.4	29.6	4.5	4.5	--

9.5.4 Specialist Recruitment and its Cost-Effect Relation

Head-hunting for specialists (Physician Recruitment) is cost-intensive in terms of offering high salaries and other benefits to attract well-known physicians to MGH or its clinics. But these measures do pay off for MGH(S) because well-known specialists attract patients.

Without active recruitment of specialists, no competent physician would voluntarily seek employment in a rural area like the Upper Peninsula.[a]

The recruitment of medical specialists benefits MGH in the way of having show-pieces.

Table 8 Specialist Recruitment

Rating of Importance(%)	Very much	Much	Undecided	Not much	Not at all
Head hunting	18.2	40.9	18.2	22.7	--
Active recruitment substantial for U. P.	6.8	20.5	43.2	20.5	6.8
Specialists as show-pieces	20.5	43.2	18.2	18.2	--

[a] This formulation shall stress the effect of a rural area vs. an urban area onto employment and living

9.5.5 Provider Alliances – Networking versus Competition

Networking, as shown in the paragraphs about Critical Access Hospitals, can have advantages for both or all sides working together. Are the networking efforts with regional competitors – like cooperatively providing services or sharing information – of MGH (like the U.P. Health Care Network, Critical Access Hospital Network etc.) pays off economically off for MGHS or do might they actually hurt MGH's economical position (the market share)? Keeping patients from seeking healthcare outside the U.P. is a benefit of networking with regional competitors in providing services and sharing information. Alliances of non-profit providers are supposed to be useful in reimbursement negotiations with governmental Medicare and Medicaid.

Table 9 Provider Alliances and Networking

Rating of Importance	Very much	Much	Undecided	Not much	Not at all
Collaboration hurts	--	2.3	18.2	50.0	29.6
Networking keeps patients within the U. P.	31.8	50.0	11.4	6.8	--
Alliances are useful for finance negotiations	38.6	38.6	11.4	6.8	4.6

9.5.6 Importance of Governmental, Public Relations and Pastoral Care

Lobby-work with politicians concerning health legislation is beneficial to hospitals like MGH.

The work of the public relation department, for example, advertising a positive image through publication or sponsoring of non-medical community events, like awarding Marquette-High-School students of excellence e.g., is believed to foster the hospital's profit margin positively.

The work of the pastoral care department has an importance within MGH's business. There is a relation between health and religion. (What kind of could be the subject of further studies in this special area)

Table 10 Governmental Relations, Marketing and Pastoral Care

Rating of Importance	Very much	Much	Undecided	Not much	Not at all
Lobby-work	29.6	50.0	18.2	2.3	--
Advertising and Image	38.6	43.2	6.8	11.4	--
Health and Religion	13.6	40.9	27.3	15.9	2.3

9.5.7 Knowledge Sharing and Communications at MGH

The MGH department heads are knowledgeable enough to answer when subordinates or customers want to know something about MGH's business/management strategy.
MGH department heads know wether subordinates are satisfied with their job. With regard to the best way of getting to know what is going on, especially on the level of plans/strategies of the upper management, there are diverse possibilities within a firm to keep up to date – employee meetings, information via email, memos etc. Information can be transmitted informally or for everyone accessible.
Informal relationships with the upper management are the best way to keep informed.

Table 11 Knowledge Sharing and Communications

Rating of Importance(%)	Very much	Much	Undecided	Not much	Not at all
Feeling competence	22.7	56.8	6.8	13.8	--
Subordinate relation	13.6	56.8	13.6	15.9	--
Informal relationships	15.9	50.0	9.1	25.0	--

9.5.8 Monetary Incentives – Effects on Performance and Satisfaction

Firms give incentives out to their employees in order to higher their performance and job-satisfaction, factors which are supposed to contribute to better outcomes in production or service delivery. But what is more important at MGH? Non-monetary incentives or monetary incentives show that the management is interested in the employees well-being and motivation.
Monetary incentives (benefits etc.) affect the work performance more than non-monetary incentives like awarding the 'employee of the months'.

The role of monetary incentives like 'result share' especially effects the employee's awareness of MGH's overall business situation not letting the employees focus on their individual interests only, like their job description and their compensation. The intention of result share can be seen besides the satisfaction – an effect, directly benefiting the employee – but also effecting him/her indirectly by tying him/her to MGH's business success and preventing him/her from doing margin harmful activities, like joining unions.

Table 12 Monetary Incentives

Rating of Importance(%)	Very much	Much	Undecided	Not much	Not at all
Money counts	13.6	50.0	9.1	22.7	4.6
ResultShare promotes the team perspective	27.3	54.5	4.6	11.4	2.3
ResultShare strengthens economical ratio	9.1	36.4	18.2	27.3	9.1

[1] Webb, C. (1999). *Win back alienated patients or face consequences, hospital leaders told.* Page.5.

[2] See Michigan Health & Hospital Association (1999). No Margin, No Mission – The Financial Realities of Michigan's Nonprofit Hopitals.

[3] Michigan Health & Hospital Association (1998). *MHA Hospital Community Benefits Survey.*

[4] Health Care Management Review (1991).

[5] Desai, K. R. et al. (1998). *Hospital Conversions from for-profit to non-profit status.*

[6] Webb, C. (1999). *Analyst: Bottom-line thinking hurts hospitals' most marketable assets.* Page 5.

[7] Webb, C. (1999). *... Bottom-line thinking hurts hospitals' most marketable assets.* Page 5.

[8] Interview MGHS-SMAUSHC-8.

[9] Interview MGHS-SMAUSHC-3.

[10] Interview MGHS-SMAUSHC-1.

[11] Interview MGHS-SMAUSHC-2.

[12] Interview MGHS-SMAUSHC-9.

[13] Interview MGHS-SMAUSHC-5.

[14] Interview MGHS-SMAUSHC-9.

[15] Interview MGHS-SMAUSHC-9.

[16] Interview MGHS-SMAUSHC-2.

[17] Interview MGHS-SMAUSHC-2.

[18] Interview MGHS-SMAUSHC-9.

[19] Interview MGHS-SMAUSHC-5.

10 Summary, Evaluation and Conclusion

... life must be understood backwards. But it must be lived forewords ...

The above repeated motto of the first page should guide the reader and help him/her to understand this thesis. It shall now also function as an orientation on how to evaluate the strategic management of MGH, especially the period between 1995 and 2000. In this work neither the view onto the past nor the view onto the present and future shall be disregarded. Therefore chapter two, three and parts of four were giving an introduction into the circumstances and impacts that formed the U.S. health care system to understand in which historical and sociological setting today's Marquette General Health System in Upper Michigan operates. However, 'the other proposition' was also paid attention to in chapters five to nine. They gave insight into the way MGHS's efforts will look like in the future. They showed that MGHS is not stuck in the past. MGHS is always concerned about how to adopt to new challenges, to prevent threats and to keep in business to offer care for the residents of the U.P. Especially in the mission statement and the comments regarding the importance of a sufficient profit margin, it is revealed that MGHS to some extent follows the guideline of steadily living forward based on a correct understanding of the past as it related to MGHS.

10.1 Summary

Now the main points – the essence – of this thesis regarding the past, present and near future of U.S. health care and MGHS will be summarized according to the questions: What can be learned generally?
What have I – what has the reader – learned out of the conducted research and the later report? And what is important to formulate the conclusion of this study?
Focusing the last years of strategic planning and development (1995 to 2000), conclusions with regard to the research propositions made in chapter one will be made that reveal my personal opinion. This leads over to my view of MGHS's

near future answering the question what MGHS could have done better in the past or might do better in the future: strengths, weaknesses, opportunities or threats will be stated. The following summarization is divided into two steps: First U.S. history, the institutional setting and management direction of MGH is pointed out; then the line of sight issue, the opinion of the certain administrative levels is highlighted in a condensed way.

10.1.1 U.S. Health Care

In the United States, the driving forces for medical service delivery in the past and still in the present rely to the bigger part on private forces than on governmental ones. And the reason, why people did not demand more governmental action on health and social issues regarding everyone in the U.S., can be seen in the immigrant mentality that remained stable over generations: First, everyone was responsible for his/her own success, taking care of one's own health and preventing negative consequences of health-endangering behavior or other outside threats. This way to look at things slightly and slowly changed over time.

The governmental part, however, became increasingly important. It was the government that broadened access to health care through the development of new payment systems besides out-of-pocket and private insurance mainly by two programs Medicare and Medicaid and others set up in the 1960s and after. However, they didn't solve the problem of under- and uninsured people.

Despite the increased action, the government had and still has a reactive character with regard to health care. If problems were and are appearing in outlines, activities were started. This is still the case today, when the federal administration is concerned about lack of access to care or cost containment. The free market, based on the individuals' initiatives, came first. The government provides more of a safety net to stop the main and worst negative outcomes effecting the general concerns of the society.

All these factors are still mirrored in today's health care system. Nevertheless, things changed on the federal level regarding the awareness of social problems and approaches to solve them in a preventive way and not only on the individual

level.[a] The U.S. health system can thus be characterized as market-based (not '-driven') with a tendency of distribution of health to the people.
The situation described above can be found in Michigan, of course, too, however, in a certain specification for this State. Marquette County, even MGH, is a micro cosmos representing the U.S. and the society representing the main facts to a certain extent.

10.1.2 Healthcare Delivery in Michigan

In Michigan health care delivery was first 'imported' by Catholic sisterhoods coming to this area from the north, from Canada. Many hospitals within Michigan reveal that religious connection to the past, when looking at their names (e.g. *St. Mary's* Hospital). Also Marquette General's history goes back to those church hospitals. Still today, church representatives and their ethical perspective are represented as memebers of the Board of Trustees.

In the beginning, Michigan's population consisted of French, English and later on of other middle-European immigrant descendants. However, the fact that the area was already settled by tribes of the native American population should not be forgotten which is still obvious in the existence of native American reservations and native American words in the public domain.
When immigrants came to this part of America in the early centuries, the country was a sparse land, urban areas and industrial centers developed first near the mines and later the locations of the steel industry.
Michigan's non-native population grew with the mining industry in the last century and then with the steel industry and the growing automotive sector which was located in the lower peninsula. Despite mining and other industry developments the Upper Peninsula remained rural.

[a] The (failed) discussion about the national health insurance, programs for minority groups, for rural areas and 'social' epidemics like AIDS.

A reason for that can be seen in the climate conditions, which do not contribute to drawing people and new industry to the Northern regions of the U.P. Since the mining industry is now decreasing, the population numbers for the U.P. are generally decreasing, too.
However, health care and education are still successfully operating industries which minimize the negative population trends to a certain extent by attracting new people (healthcare professionals and students) to the area. But, there still is the lack of productive industry ventures in opposition to primary service industries. Since the latter depends on the number of residents, being their customers and providing future margins, the U.P. is and still will be under the pressure of declining or low birth rates. Out-migration and growing numbers of the elderly pose a threat to the area in the future.

All these impacts are effecting healthcare delivery and hospital providers and the way they do business in the U.P. of Michigan. Certain specific forces and regulations with regard to health care delivery formed the healthcare providers and their service range besides above mentioned impacts.

Michigan's specifics in legislation also played a role. One of those specifics shall be repeated here again, explaining on the basis of the U.P. health care market how the theoretical approaches to economical theories in health care contributed to the development and the service lines of MGHS under the Michigan legislative situation: Michigan is under CON-legislation. This is to contain costs in healthcare (which was as known the case in all States since the early 1900s and especially after World War II.)

Regulation was the main vehicle to contain rising healthcare costs in the 1970s. The 1980s and 1990s were the decades of implementation of market forces through retraction of CON-legislation in some States – not in Michigan – accompanied by growing managed care or the promotion of increased advertising of service advantages certain providers may have had through the enactment of anti-trust-laws; providers 'had' to compete more than before when some regulatory laws made existing facilities safe of new competitors capturing market shares in a region.

The situation in Michigan's U.P., however, was different. Managed care never developed much. Market forces like competition were increased or 'exported into' the U.P. via providers of neighboring states: Patients were willing to travel greater distances to receive healthcare, and so a larger amount of providers was finally competing for the 300,000 U.P. residents. This competitive impact on U.P. hospitals like MGH was also strengthened by tougher reimbursement politics by governmental programs or private insurance. Despite the Certificate-of-Need program, other market-based cost-control methods like DRG-payments or the 1997 Balanced Budget Act with the implementation of managed-care options in Medicare and Medicaid coverage are still in force in Michigan.

10.1.3 Healthcare Management by MGH

With regard to the situation of MGH in the last decades it can be said that MGH could use the CON-regulation to strengthen its prime position under the group of medical providers in the U.P. Managed-Care density was low in the U.P., new competitors had some difficulties to enter the Michigan U.P. market in terms of opening new facilities because those needed CON-approval. The already existing provider MGH could thus relatively undisturbedly expand by purchasing already existing clinics. This was made possible by the fact, that MGH as the largest provider had the most sufficient financial resources.

Nevertheless, as said before, there were competitors of MGH/MGHS in the neighboring States, and also smaller competitors within the U.P.

In the 1990s, especially cost containment and keeping the flow of patients on a sufficient level, was high on the agenda. To answer these threats and other impacts endangering MGH's financial health, MGH was the main driving force of setting up a U.P. health care network to cope with increased market-consequences with collaborative type of arrangements in opposition to attempts to out-compete other providers within the U.P. that patients seek health care within the U.P.

Summarizing the strategic management efforts and activities of MGH within the last decades, one could say that before 1995, Marquette General Hospital grew externally by broadening the service range and broadening geographic access to care and specialty treatment in general. A growth strategy was partly substituted and completed by a stability strategy. The emphasis on the latter was also the guideline for the following years, as shown by the strategic efforts made in the late 1990s.

After 1995, the plan was to develop into an integrated delivery system to react to a changing healthcare environment. The goal was to grow externally, while at the same time including more different types of health service offerings and co-operating with former competitors.
The target point of the 1996 strategic plan was: Integration of different services in one hand; not so much increasing in terms of quantity, but increase in efficiency; maintaining an adequate flow of patients and fighting back tougher reimbursement rates.

In MGH's management process in the late 1990s, however, the strategic plan of 1995 played only a minor role. Apart from the cooperative approaches accompanying the role as the main referral center, the medical center of the U.P., this plan did too much discuss and recommend topics that actually weren't so high on the agenda in the U.P. An example as assumed by the consultants is that of managed care and its impact on the diverse areas and levels of health service delivery in the U.P.
Other issues, like employee relations (the connection between satisfaction, participation and compensation, etc.) were not stressed at all. Also the specific role of institutional MGH's history, the status of a non-profit provider and the corresponding task of respecting community needs was not sufficiently paid attention to. The hospital took its own way partially related to the strategic plan of 1996 which is discussed further down.
What MGH did after 1995 was to update technical equipment; to invest in new buildings; and to proceed in telehealth operations, important to attract customers

and to highlight MGH as the Regional Referral Center which is able to deliver all kinds of services.
The set up of the Critical Access Hospital Network, collaborative behavioral health service arrangements, new ventures like founding an assisted living facility or designing an insurance plan – both ways of strategic piggybacking – in cooperation with the physician community and with the intention were a decisive step into the future. Thus it was ensured to keep an adequate flow of customers and patients, containing out-migration, and securing the stream of revenue in an environment of cost control and decreasing reimbursement rates. Health care within the U.P. was stream-lined. This corresponds with the theoretic outcomes of strategic alliances and the other concepts within organizational theory outlined in chapter 5.

The efficient delivery of services was also promoted by starting and/or expanding telehealth applications and an information technology system to connect the diverse providers within the U.P. Health Care Network more easily. To stress MGH's interest of collaboration, the physicians as customers were asked to give their input in the planning of the EKG-network, feedback about their concerns regarding referral mechanisms etc. The other group of customers, the patients, was paid attention to by studies checking their awareness, expectations and concerns.
It showed that patients are recognizing MGH/MGHS as 'the' central location to go to for health care.

MGH was steadily aware of controlling the institutional functions and outlook, not only the image was tested, also 'hard facts,' like medical records and expenditures were reviewed. Inside and outside the institution everything should be working fine. Therefore, the human resource department also developed a new compensation plan, including the monthly payments and insurance plus a result share. The latter plan completed the already existing pay for performance.
Both tried to increase motivation and performance by giving monetary incentives for corresponding employees. Result Share however, combined the interest of the hospital

- to make the employees aware of the 'entire' business success, of all factors contributing to the overall hospital margin and not only of what the single employee gains and,
- to find a way of way of compensation where monetary extra-benefits are tied or related to the extra-margin. Only money that was earned by the hospital before can also be referred to the employees.

These two intentions were brought up by one administrator in an interview and also confirmed in a certain way by the department heads, when asked to rate the effect of monetary incentives like Result Share. The large majority of over 50 percent has seen an effect on the employee's awareness of MGH's overall business situation, also an effect in tying the employees or group of employees to MGH's business success and preventing them from doing 'harmful' activities, like joining union campaigns.

The last years of this second millennium were a time for 'growing internally' by improving quality and preparing for the future. MGH was growing up, the major institutional goals of growth of the 'juvenile times' of MGH were becoming saturated, now it was time to look for partners to secure, what was already reached and earned, stability before growth was high on the strategic agenda.

10.2 The Line of Sight at MGH

After analyzing what was planned, done and reached at MGH in the main parts of this thesis and in the last paragraph, it is now also important to look at the line of sight. This expression stands for the question, if all levels of management which were involved in the decision-making process do have the same or at least a corresponding opinion regarding the business strategy of the last five years.

As fully pointed out already in the last chapters, this strategy has to incorporate

- the main strengths

    as the large service range, the quality of physicians and care delivery and the position of being on the cutting edge of technology strengthened through the network activities, the good financial health and a high morale employee force which all contributed to a good name recognition with the customer population;

- the main weaknesses

  as the low and decreasing population density within the U.P., the great distances that have to be overcome by the outreach physicians, the tightness of space for further expansions within the Marquette campus and the difficulties in recruiting good people to the rural U.P.;
- the main opportunities

  as the potential to further increase market share, where it is still low, the strong information technology to link service providers and users within the U.P. to streamline care delivery and at last vertical integration of new services like the U.P. Health Plan, which is making MGH independent from other companies or programs and includes at the same time also the potential to offer joined insurance plans e.g. in cooperation with Blue Cross/Blue Shield in the U.P. and;
- the main threats for MGH's business success

  as increasing regional competition drawing customers out of the U.P.

  decreasing reimbursement through changes in governmental programs

When asked to evaluate the last years' strategy, the strategy that was best coping with above mentioned factors and situation the Assistant Administrators came to following overall rating.

1.) The strategy component 'interlocking arrangements, cooperation between hospitals, physicians and insurance plans' was seen as most important and rated as the number one issue. 'Increasing capital assets, vertical integration/extension of services, promoting quality of staff and services' and 'seeking political support' was mostly rated as being equally important and interchangeable taking the second important position after the cooperation as the number one. However, some additionally prioritized the three following issues:

2.) 'quality promotion of staff and services' was actually cited second,

3.) 'vertical integration' as third important and

4.) 'seeking political support' fourth often.

In questionnaires, the department heads and program directors were asked to rate indicator statements which were related with the four strategy components above to get to know, how they rate the general importance of those issues for a business strategy of MGH. Comparing the results, one can conclude afterwards, if this level of management is thinking that they agreed to the chosen direction of management at MGH/MGHS, if it was accepted and understood or not.

The cooperation of hospitals, physicians and insurance plans was seen as most decisive and the right thing to do by the overwhelming majority of the respondents. Also with regard to the natural importance of ongoing increase in capital assets, correspondence through the department heads' rating with MGH's business strategy was reached.
Renovated facilities and updated technology were seen as crucial, but not as important as internal customer-magnets as excellent services.
The opinion that excellent service provision pays off, can also be found in the clear results for training of all employees in their field regarding specialty treatment and nursing, management issues, customer friendliness etc. It was thought that high-trained staff also prevents from seeking healthcare at competitors.
This goes in line with the fact that advertising a positive image to secure the profit margin of MGHS scored with the highest percentages of all results besides the cooperation issue. Public relations at MGH thus needs to highlight internal show-pieces like excellent services seen as very beneficial for MGHS' image in the population.
And because of these internal show-pieces in form of the services also the medical specialists providing such services were also seen as important for the overall image of MGHS. That is why a lot of the respondents probably agreed to the other side of that, too: The high costs MGHS has to take into account for specialist head-hunting are paying off for the majority of the respondents.
Also, the related area of governmental relations was more often rated as important for MGH than material focus-points a business strategy should include.

Vertical integration/addition of new services is also seen as having positive effects on streamlining health care delivery in the sense of enabling the hospital to meet the customers' demands more efficiently with a negative impact on the quality of particular services.
However, asking especially about the strategic potential of the U.P. Health Plan, when remembering the Finance Officer's words and what own insurance products are all about, a large part of the department head level did not know if adding of new services like insurance products would make MGH less dependent on the governmental sources of income. However, offering own insurance might be a relief and an answer to the governmental programs providing over 50% of revenue share for the hospital and steadily increasing the reimbursement rates.
With regard to specialist recruiting and its cost-effect-relation for MGH, a relatively large group of 18.2 percent did not know what to answer in combination with a respectively large amount of positive and negative answers.
This kind of distribution shows that the department heads maybe didn't know about the strategic background these topics have for MGH. This, which was right for benefits of 'self-owned insurance' and 'specialist-recruiting, doesn't have to be a strategic problem, but could be understood as need for background education besides the training of primary work tasks.
When looking at the 'don't know, what to answer' shares within the entire rating, some of them can, as explained before, taken as demand for education to strengthen the broader understanding of how strategic plans, all-day-business at MGH and health care politics are interrelating with each other.

The area of communication and employee compensation within the department head survey reveals how educational offers and firm internal communication are rated by the department heads. Probabaly in this context there is to be seen a need that should have been and has to be respected in the business strategy of MGH.
In general, the majority of department heads feel knowledgeable enough what to answer when subordinates or customers request information about MGH' business/management strategy. This fits to the distribution for the other topics: the

'don't know-fraction' was always the minority fraction compared with the ones that had a positive or negative opinion.
However, it is a large minority if 10% of all still feel insecure with some questions which required some background knowledge.
Perhaps the way communication functions at MGH offers an explanation. The overwhelming majority of department heads think that using informal contacts with the upper management is the best way to keep updated about upper management plans. The minority, who does not agree to that point, might prefer formal information via open meetings etc. and accesible to everyone. Probly the 10%-minority is group of people who do not have informal opportunities.
This stresses the point that there could exist a need to steadily increase processes of knowledge-sharing and communication through directed methods, which do not depend on informal contacts. Ways of formal communication could be round-letters, staff meetings and ways of the participation of lower hierarchy levels in decision-making.

10.3 Evaluation of the Thesis' Research Propositions

This paragraph will check the propositions made in the beginning of this thesis which represent my interest to answer the underlying research question:

How does strategic planning of a U.S. rural non-profit health care provider look like in the tense relationship of ethic mission, and economic margin?

Propositions:

1.) Marquette General Health System's main goal as a non-profit provider is to focus primarily the ethical mission and secondly the economic margin, and this shows in their business activity, community relations before asset management etc.
2.) The location in the US-market economy and society's individualized mentality, make socially responsible health care provision impossible.
3.) Between the upper and lower management level, clear differences about what the overall business policy and strategy should be like, are

supposed to exist, where the upper management is supposed to follow more rational principles to 'keep the system economically running' and the lower management being closer to the customer patient's needs and 'what is best for the help-seeking individual,'

4.) Especially the activities within the area of marketing in an American hospital are interesting to learn from for German hospital providers facing a tendency towards increased market forces changing the face of hospital management and service delivery. German health care providers could adopt the American ability to do business in the tense relationship between ethical and economic demands.

The first hypothesis does not correspond with the reality of Marquette General Health System. At Marquette General Health System, the bottom line is to look at a sufficient margin as a way to stay in business. And despite this margin-orientation, there is no intention to convert to a for-profit status or to give up the mission-orientated way to deliver health care by serving all residents of the region with no exclusion of people being too poor to pay for their service. Making internal profit and thus taking care that the hospital focuses those areas which are promising to open up new and large sources of revenue like the nursing home business in a community with growing numbers of older people is an intelligent thing to do. This was the idea the majority of administrators had in mind, when rating margin versus mission as follows.

Both were seen important by the administrators as part of MGH's business strategy, however with a certain emphasis: Margin was seen as most critical for MGH and cited twice as much as the opinion that 'no mission, no margin' could be taken as a motto for the management of this non-profit hospital within the last five years.

Putting margin orientation before mission goals can be good for a phase like the last years, where MGH had to take care in order to secure its financial health after having expanded and finished new constructions.

In general, however, and for the future, especially for a future, when at a certain point the phase of institutional growth is definitely finished, it might be dangerous to put margin first for a longer period of time. Mission is the more decisive factor.

Customers seek health care at MGHS facilities because they think that this provider is different. Perhaps it is the nearest available service provider, but in many cases it will be also the preferred provider because of its service line and because of its image. With regard to the image, also the service offerings are decisive, but that is not all. Image is more. It is the added value of a hospital, soft factors that make customer chose this hospital, and even it is not the nearest and even a competitor offers the same services. And this added value is incorporated in a good hospital mission. Why is it important to stress the difference between a hospital services and these other factors in making people decide where to go?

What is MGHS doing under its perspective when competitors, for example the bigger providers from the neighboring regions on the state lines or from Lower Michigan, are working as efficient as MGHS, and are as much increasing their capital assets, what is generally easy to do, as long they have paying customers? What happens when all competitors are claiming to have an updated technology, to have excellent services? And of course, they will try to claim that. Who would say the opposite?

Despite the fact that a margin is obviously important if you want to stay in business and can't be neglected like by the Mercy Health System in Detroit, to a non-profit provider, as outlined in chapter nine, it is not 'most' important. The most important factor in management of a hospital is to work for a unique image, something that makes the hospital different and distinguishable for a patient.

Reaching that positive difference by offering highest amount of MRI procedures or by having the shiniest patient rooms is not the right way because there will be the day when other providers will have purchased a newer technical equipment or will have renovated their facilities and then, MGH will partly fall back again for a certain time. These differences might not last for a long time and it is expensive to be always and in every category to be on the absolute cutting edge of technology

Only built firmly trust on side of the patients which developed over a long period of time promises to maintain a positive patient-provider connection. The positive connection can only be kept by constantly building trust. In this context, it is of vital importance for the hospital to reflect the ethical mission to the public.

Probably the department being nearer to the patient concerns and demands knew this difference and that is why they rated the position and the work of public relations at MGHS as so important, more important than increasing capital assets or vertical integration of services. The knew about the importance of attracting customers by more than just excellent services.

The second proposition does not reflect MGHS the way it was and still is. In times of my internship and before the following research stays, I initially had the 'wrong' picture of the U.S. in mind: a totaly capitalistic economical system with the respective outcomes for the society and the individual. But: Market systems are not always those systems are not always pure and clear as described in the political theory. For example, with regard to health care, meritorious intentions lead to health care planning and later to health care distribution in order to fight back market outcomes like rising costs. In Michigan CON-legislation keeps the free market system under control.

Thus the first conclusion with regard to this proposition is: The forces effecting MGHS and business are not totally demand-supply-driven. From the governmental perspective, the principle of socially just access to care is also paid attention to. In conclusion, the underlying point of the hypothesis that market driven health care and socially responsible health care are two expressions which never fit together cannot be kept up because the market-driven health care system in the U.S. has already changed into a nowadays more market-based system including regulatory approaches.

On the institutional level or the community level, socially responsible health care is possible (as shown in the hospital mission of many community hospitals since John Hopkins and now MGHS committed to provide uncompensated care.) This social responsibility is ensured by cross subsidization on the hospital finance level. The hospitals needs to make a margin to finance health services delivered to the poor and indigent of the population (See chapter nine).

However, in the U.S. system, one problem remains: Initiatives based on the community level or private efforts might work out in an area, like the U.P., with a low population density. In metropolitan areas, however, where in some parts the number of needy people is higher than the amount of wealthy people providing the necessary revenue to a hospital to offer charitable care, such a system can have an socially unjust character. As shown in the example of Mercy Health System in Detroit, socially responsible health care provision depends on a sufficient margin. Thus socially responsible health care provision is possible in a market-based environment, but is not guaranteed and it depends on wether there are enough patients – demanding health care and being able to pay for it – which are the sources of the hospital's margin used for cross-subsidization of uncompensated care.

A reminder at this point: This work has certain boundaries. That is why the above mentioned conclusions regarding issues of social responsibility and justice in health care delivery, can't go into such depth, since my work is not observing 'the' U.S. situation, it is limited to the extent of the single-case MGHS in the Upper Peninsula of Michigan. The general U.S. situation functions as a matrix providing the general background.
The conclusion with regard to this proposition has to be understood in the way that market-based health care does not mean, as people used to systems of 'socialized medicine' maybe think, that 'all' healthcare providers are forced to focus only profitable risks instead of respecting the needs of the whole community population.

Regarding the third proposition and the question if there are really huge differences in what strategic management at MGHS should look like in general, it can be said: When summarizing the results of the comparison of the ranking of strategic issues or components for a overall business strategy, it can be concluded that lower and higher levels of management at MGH generally pulled together

with regard to their awareness of decisive strategy components and with regard to a general priority.
Only one additional point has to be made. It is about the role and the importance of community relations and marketing. The area of activity was rated more important by the department heads and program directors than the importance assigned by the administrators, when looking at their priority listing. Public relations played and play a more decisive role than just the fourth position on the ranking of activities: They have to be considered for an general business strategy. Like taking care of the capital assets, taking care of customer awareness and community relations is seen as a bottom-line of strategic management.

The fourth proposition is discussed in the last, the eleventh chapter.

10.4 Strategic Management at MGHS: The Past, the Present, the Future

MGHS is doing well, they have a large market share and the central position within the group of regional health care providers as the referral center/the medical center, they stay on the cutting edge of technology, have a high performing and high morale staff – obvious also in not having any further successful unionization campaigns and strikes – and also the management is pulling together with regard to the direction MGHS should take. This promising situation of economical and regional success was reached not by chance or by any potentially worse management of competing, providers; it was, as already mentioned by the Board's Secretary, the reward for smart management and the fact that all levels of management and the employee force were pulling together. The latter becomes clear in the voting against unionization of the hospital (against third party players additionally sitting on the labor negotiation table). It is intelligent to stabilize the earned success by building cooperative types of arrangements and efforts that strengthen the employee's relation to their employer (understandable and motivational compensation plans and participation, communication and studies checking the employee opinion).

However, this kind of strategy should be paid attention to and the issue of authenticity besides being on the prime technological and regional position should not be forgotton.
That means two things: Authenticity through looking at the non-profit status, hospital mission and the hospital's history as a market good, something that is not only of added value, but of central value, the unmistakable face of MGHS compared with other hospitals in the region which are- also other non-profit institutions. Therefore, the position of mission has to come first and all other management tasks which are definitely also important have be put on the same or the second place, but before. This refers to the institutional theory pointed out in chapter 5. Organizational functioning is heavily influenced by prevailing norms, values and beliefs. Sometimes, not the right beliefs are followed (see gag rules, chapter 5). At MGHS, there is a tendency within the administration to focus on margin as prime management guideline. However, MGHS has a non-profit status, a certain history and correspondingly, a good mission. Why not put this fact which represents MGHS's character, first in marketing and management? (See also arguments of the last paragraph)
This conclusion corresponds with the hypothesis of the consultant Mr Wong 'No mission, no mark up.' In the case of MGHS there can be stated: No mission, no future.

Authenticity can also be reached by looking more critically at the development of an integrated delivery system, the underlying advantages, disadvantages and accompanying demands.
Without developing a corporate identity which provides medical service, nursing home services, and insurance products, the hospital might lose name recognition which can only be gained if a provider is not only large, but also of special and excellent standard. MGHS will have to face the danger of providing more and different services, but at the end maybe only average services, which are not seen as outstanding in comparison with the services of competitors by the customers.
The more various service offerings MGHS integrates, the more difficulties it will have and will have to face the challenge of having them all on the cutting

edge of technology, service quality or efficiency. Looking for example only at the structure of the car industry, especially former Daimler-Benz, an obvious tendency of giving up former strategies of broadening the service range towards telecommunications and services becomes clear. Now the focus is on company-merging like in the case of Daimler-Benz and Chrysler in order to stay competitive on the world market. Nowadays DaimlerChrysler only offer those products for which they are known experts for.

Transferring that to MGHS, there can be seen the threat for MGHS that their customers not knowing anymore what makes MGHS unique and outstanding in terms of excellence. If MGHS is offering 'anything and everything,' the customers might lose the trust in MGHS's excellence and specialties, and MGHS lose its corporate identity and its image in the population.

Therefore, marketing and education are areas of importance for the hospital. The more regional competition increases, marketing should take care of what customers should know about MGHS and how customers are benefiting from all the structural changes that come along with that. Education then is important to make the own employees ambassadors of the hospital's unique brand, being modern, working efficiently and that all with the prime goal to serve the customer in the special mission-orientated way. And the more regional competition rises, personal factors make the difference why somebody is seeking healthcare locally because he or she knows the institution or somebody from MGHS and feels that they are committed to what they are doing.

Another point of criticism can be made regarding the way of delivering pastoral care at MGHS. There is no question that this is generally a good thing, it is part of the image and tradition of this hospital. However, having the chaplains on staff might be problematic according my point of view. Taking the unionization campaigns as an example, it is potentially not clear wether all employees and staff members of MGHS have a corresponding opinion pro or contra. If now the chaplains are on the payroll list of the hospital and if this is additionally organizationally biased, because of the chaplaincy department being part of the hospital's administrative level and under supervision by an administrator, it is not obvious for the single employee on which side 'the church' in the hospital is standing. I would guess that everybody who needs it will get spiritual support. But is

hard to say if that is the really the case, since the chaplaincy department is organizationally positioned and financially depending on the hospital (administration). It is understandable why the position of pastoral care lies on the side of the hospital in the U.S. It has to do with the legislative and institutional status of U.S. churches and congregations. A joint approach to finance and manage spiritual support/pastoral care in public hospitals is so not very much likely because of the higher grade of religious splitting.
That means for pastoral care at MGHS to be aware of the danger of being opinionated or management-depending. Especially, when conflict situations within the staff and employee force of MGHS arise, the chaplains need to do everything to stay neutral. They should be open to welcome everyone and ready to settle conflicts and to help the people to eventually reconcile with others.

Of course, there are also hard factors besides those smooth factors of human relations and behavior to make MGHS an attractive customer magnet with a special brand. Such a factor is the use of information technology and telehealth applications. This is a means of transporting how up to date MGHS really is to the clients.
However, much more interesting from the management or the economical point of view is the use of such technology for improved rural health care access in areas like the U.P. Why not try sell 'healthcare by MGHS' with its specifics as an additional product to interested other health care managers in seminars, video-conferences etc.? The Walt Disney Corporation did something comparable by founding the Walt Disney Institute to sell their way of customer service, called Guestology, to other institutions (from telecommunications to health care etc.). The product 'selling their own way of doing it' provides Walt Disney with an additional source of revenue besides the original one through offering amusement to people.
Neither in the case of Walt Disney nor in the potential case of MGHS offerings, this would endanger the clear understanding of what MGHS is doing, as critically observed above, when discussing the disadvantages of too large and diversified providers because education, management training would only help to get

a better understanding of MGHS product and background and how they do mission orientated business.
There would be one decisive advantage because this would bring another kind of customer to the U.P. However, the winter climate conditions are again a disadvantage to attract people.
Trying to offer excellent service and to highlight the own image, accompanied by keeping technically up to date and financial-structurally up to date by networking is, what MGHS is already doing well.
However, following Kierkegaard and his motto, strategic management at MGHS should mean to live life forward in the above mentioned way and never underestimate care guided by the hospital mission.

For the local customer, this very philosophy and the long-standing history of the hospital are definitely the crucial factors which determine the genuine character and brand name of MGHS.

11 Learning Aspects

> "Twenty years ago, management was a 'dirty word' for those involved in nonprofit organizations. It meant business, and nonprofits priced themselves on being free of the taint of commercialism and above such social considerations as the bottom-line. Now, most of them have learned that nonprofits need management more than business does, precisely because they lack the discipline of the bottom-line."[1]

11.1 Strategic Learning Aspects for German Non-Profit Organizations

What can German readers, what could German health care providers in the area of tax-exempted non-profit health care delivery learn from strategic management at MGHS and the U.S. health care environment?

The fourth proposition of this thesis – that the German side *can* learn something – is now evaluated within these last paragraphs based on the quote cited above which, as the author believes, is right for both sides

The according conclusion is: There are ways of delivering social healthcare while working profitably and visa versa. And that is what is also interesting for German hospital and health service providers to know. Community needs and margin-focused care delivery can go hand in hand, if 'efficiency' is not seen as revealed in the statement below, which is characterizing kind of the direction and the fear within the debate about health care delivery and the right strategy in the German system:

> "In times of increasing scarcity of public managed sources [because of rising prices/costs and decreasing tax revenue with regard to population wide health insurance] the public debate has changed its direction and is becoming more simplified adopting economical ratio as a way to get around the more complicated, money and time wasting-process of seeking a consensus with regard to new priorities in the way how to serve the social [the health] needs within the German society.
>
> The term of 'needs' being high on the agenda within the public discourse is replaced by the magic formula of 'efficiency'."[2]

11.2 Learning Aspect: Efficiency-Need-Merit Relation

However, when looking at the efforts of MGHS with regard to marketing and community relations, it shows that 'community needs/public weal' and 'efficiency' are not contrary terms. Efficiency and margin-orientation are the necessary tool to satisfy community needs and demands for merit health care possible. Advertising the hospital, highlighting the medical experts on staff as stars and through setting up community ties and cooperation with other hospitals to promote name recognition and to gain efficient collaboration to stay alive in markets becoming more regional – these all are management issues that are done to reach both goals, first efficiency and then the prime goal of a non-profit provider: Welfare for all residents of the surrounding community and region.

The collaborative aspect is what German non-profit providers in general could learn from and adopt in general from the U.S. setting. Specifically the way MGHS collaborates with former competitors and the way legislation tries to serve the population by promoting critical access facility networks around regional medical centers have promising potentials for German health care providers. They are also fighting with issues like cost containment and changes in the health care service delivery: Health care markets in and around Germany are changing. The government placed a cup on discretionary spending. Nowadays only the most cost efficient or simply cheapest medical services (medical treatment and pharmaceuticals) are paid for by national health insurance. Additionally, private coinsurance becomes a growing market, filling the gap of service coverage in these areas, where this service is no longer covered by national health insurance. And there is a good base of people in the country who are not wealthy enough to subscribe for total private insurance, but able to pay for coinsurance for specialty procedures or special benefits like treatment by specialists, in-hospital care.

This market partially substituting the governmental driving force (in case of the national health insurance) contributes to a tendency towards general primary care to everyone and specialty care, dental surgery, orthopedics, for the those who have sufficient private insurance or coinsurance added to their national health insurance.

Before discussing learning aspects limited to German (non-profit or) public utility providers, first one general aspect is pointed out. It is the existence and the promotion of a referral network between primary care physicians in the country side working together with the specialty facilities of MGH in Marquette by referring patients.
These physicians function as gatekeepers deciding how necessary eventual special treatment or secondary care is. As mentioned by various interviewed persons, it became clear that strengthening a voluntary and strong connection is one decisive management task. It is a corner-stone of Marquette General Health System compared. It stresses the point of collaboration as a way to efficiently operate in an environment of cost reimbursement with a tendency to become tighter over the years.

11.3 Learning Aspect: Referral Networks

Referral networks could be an interesting contribution to the German discussion on how to switch to a gatekeeper model of health care delivery, where health care is based on the primary service of primary care physicians and referrals to specialty care facilities are made if needed. What are the facts deducted from MGHS that make a referral system function?

There is a provider network with a medical center having the clear prime position within the range of neighboring providers. In rural areas with a low density of population, the residents often live far distanced to the main medical facilities with a broad range of service offerings in specialties (e.g. in the State of Mecklenburg-Vorpommern, the region of Upper Palatine in the Freestate of Bavaria or the region of the Eifel in the State of Rhineland-Palatine). There, the switch to such a referral system might be a positive thing: Patients are recommended to go to specialty facilities after a primary care physician has provided the necessary primary medical service and has checked the need for any further specialty treatment in a tight and two-way collaboration with the referral center, the hospital.

The important point and the difference is not the referral issue. That is what also Germans know because patients covered by the public national health insurance always need a referral of a primary care physician to receive in-hospital care or specialty treatment. The important point I want to stress is: In the U.S. healthcare system, you find interesting regional networks and partnerships where the different providers know the other side and each other's interests. Each side is informed about what is going on with their patients, and in the practices and administrations. Referral physicians and referral centers work together closely to safe resources, to work cost-efficiently and to optimize patient care and access to care.

It is a partnership and not only a legislatively based referral connection. This could be promoted by legislative incentives to strengthen referral physician-hospital relationships/partnerships like in the U.P. of Michigan with the Critical Access Hospital Network initiated by State legislation or the voluntary iniative of the U.P. Health Care Network. In German areas like Upper Palatine in the South or Vorpommern in the North, increased governmental support for existing or for the development of voluntary referral networks could secure access to healthcare for rural areas.[a]

[a] In that sense, this is a different perspective to look at the access issue because in the U.S., the emphasiz is not only on securing access, but on improving access. In Germany it is more a matter of keeping the standards of access as high as possible. This dates back to the times of a socialized medicine and to the time when there were sufficient financial resources for health care in Western and Eastern Germany which is not as much the case today.

11.4 Learning Aspect: Mission-Marketing Relation

In my view, the tendency towards increased implementation of market forces into the system of socialized medicine does have some implications especially for German non-profit providers that result in situations that are comparable with American disproportional share and nonprofit hospitals. Only those hospitals which have a certain mission are willing to get their revenues primarily by patients under the national health insurance. In return they face the consequence of tied reimbursement because most of their patients are not those private patients who pay higher rates per procedure. Loss in terms of the revenue is also reached by more ambulatory services substituting services based on hospitalization. Thus the primary goal even of a mission-orientated hospital provider is to gain (wealthier private) patients to secure the stream of revenue.

All these threats have to be answered by economical approaches to gain efficiency like mentioned above and increased efforts to highlight the things a certain non-profit provider is doing well. Even in a system of still existing socialized medicine, there are differences between a hospital committed to serve the needs of a surrounding community and hospitals that see no need to focus on any activities which do not primarily contribute to a margin. According to that, one could think on the one hand of alliances and networks between the certain public or church-affiliated hospitals within a city like Hanover, its region or others, cooperating with regard to service delivery and specialist recruitment. On the other hand, one could think of how to highlight the advantages of their kind of health care delivery in a growing competition between all providers to attract patients, the source of all margin and revenue. And here especially marketing comes into play.

From former study experiences in Germany I hold the opinion that too many especially church affiliated non-profit providers look at competition and financial realities like a rabbit watching the snake. This is based on an understanding that morality and market behavior don't fit together. Or they simply neglect the existence of market forces. These hospitals can learn how important marketing is in a competitive market situation in terms of fighting for well paying patients to secure their kind of mission statement to serve the patient in a more complete understanding, including spiritual and social health, no matter if that is all profitable in particular for the hospital or not and not primarily guided by the health insurance recommended treatment policies. My point of view is that mission-orientation and margin-orientation go hand in hand. Non-profit hospitals first need their mission as the 'shining marketing star' to attract patients and to earn a sufficient margin to stay in business. The sufficient margin enables them to reinvest money into mission-orientied activities.

11.4.1 'Tue Gutes und sprich darüber'

The above headline's meaning 'Do good things and talk about it' contains the aspect which is still not common in the nonprofit-orientated sector in Germany, especially when there are any roots in the religious environment, no matter if hospitals or other service areas. Advertising is based on the idea that one company is doing better than another and that aspect contradicts Christian norms and values.

Nevertheless, advertising and lobbying; targeting customers, politicians and sponsors, that is, what even hospitals, like church hospitals have to do a lot more to make people aware of what they are doing, what they are doing differently and why, and at last, how these efforts pay off for customers to answer the question:

Why should someone go to a church-affiliated provider instead of going to the nearby larger medical university hospital or if possible, to the small specialty (day) clinic owned by a private investor group? Since physician advertisement is not allowed in Germany, especially most of the diverse non-direct methods of community relations and marketing at MGHS to promote name recognition are interesting. However, the precondition for those activities is the legality with regard to anti-trust-laws and the still tight permission to advertise in the German medical care market.

Apart from the mentioned effects active marketing of the mission-orientation could have on the outside of the hospital, it is supposed to be also helpful for the

internal side: for the employee relations. To formulate a clear mission-statement as in the example of MGHS could not only provide a good orientation for the employees, but could also increase their motivation and their commitment to the hospital. Working for an institution with high moral standards is supposed to make employees more proud of working for this institution.
This commitment which means taking care of the community needs based on merit also leads to less employee-employer-conflicts with regard to compensation issues, for example. Having to take care of mission standards may makes employees put their own and personal issues (compensation etc.) on the second place, their job, if they are working for high moral and mission-based healthcare provision comes first.
Thus stressing the point of mission-commitment of this institution could function as a kind of non-monetary incentive in order to ensure the moral based service and kind of an additional non-monetary compensation through a high-moral work environment: Pride (because of working at this place) instead of money.

For German providers it is the attitude of U.S. non-profit providers how to cope with realities and how to promote themselves which could be drawn from this thesis. You cannot set moral standards if you do not apply economical ratio in the market environment, advertising what you offer and show the benefits to the people, customers and the employees. Market-based health care, as showed with MGHS, is not totally margin-driven and even incorporates opposite efforts.
Furthermore, there would be no need to worry for any provider committed to the public need to die in the future if any 'Americanization' of the German health care system proceeded (the tendency of adopting trends). If such a trend went on as before in other areas of the (healthcare) business or the society, it would become more important to look at questions like how to prepare for such a change and which tools to apply to cope with the new challenges.

---

[1] Drucker, P. F. (July/August 1989). *What business can learn from nonprofits?* Page 89.

[2] Blanke, Bernhard (1994). *'Governance' im Gesundheitswesen (Governance in the health system).* Page 15.

Appendix

Table 13 U.S. Health Expenditures and Socioeconomic Indicators

Item	1960	1970	1980	1990	1993	1995	1997	1999
National health expenditures ($ billions)	26.9	73.2	247.3	699.4	898.5	993.7	1092.4	1228.5
National health expenditures in percent of GDP	5.1	7.1	8.9	12.2	13.7	13.7	13.5	13.9
National health expenditures per capita ($ billions)	142	341	1052	2689	3350	3638	3927	4340
GDP ($ billions)	527	1036	2784	5744	6558	7270	8111	8845
CPI on 1984 basis	n / a	0.390	0.829	1.290	1.421	1.498	1.576	1.627
U.S. population (millions)	190	215	235	260	268	273	278	283
U.S. population, age less than 65 years	n / a	194	209	228	235	239	243	248
U.S. population, age 65 and older	n / a	21	26	32	34	34	35	35

Source: Health Care Financing Administration (2000). *National Health Expenditures Projections Table 1*. This index lists data based on the 1997 version – the latest release – of the national health expenditures projections from November 1998.
The 1970 to 1999 figures are adjusted to the 1960 figures' decimal point by rounding. The 1960 data is from the HCFA index of the *National Health Expenditures Aggregate, Table 09*.

Table 14 U.S. Health Expenditures Aggregate Amounts (in $ billions)

Type of Expenditure	1960	1970	1980	1990	1993	1995	1997	1998
National Health	26.9	73.2	247.3	699.4	898.5	993.3	1088.2	1049.1
Health Services/Supplies	25.2	67.9	235.6	674.8	869.5	962.5	1053.5	1113.7
Personal Health Care	23.6	63.8	217.0	614.7	790.5	879.1	968.6	1019.3
Hospital Care	9.3	28.0	102.7	256.4	323.0	347.0	370.2	382.8
Physician Services	5.3	13.6	45.2	146.3	185.9	201.9	217.8	229.5
Dental Services	2.0	4.7	13.3	31.6	39.5	45.0	51.1	53.8
Other Profess. Services	0.6	1.4	6.4	34.7	46.1	53.6	61.5	66.6
Home Health Care	0.1	0.2	2.4	13.1	23.0	29.1	30.5	29.3
Drugs/Non-Durables	4.2	8.8	21.6	59.9	76.2	88.6	108.6	121.9
Prescriptive Drugs	2.7	5.5	12.0	37.7	50.6	61.0	78.5	90.6
Vision Products/Durables	0.6	1.6	3.8	10.5	12.3	13.3	15.1	15.5
Nursing Home Care	0.8	4.2	17.6	50.9	66.4	75.5	84.7	87.8
Other Pers. Health Care	0.7	1.3	4.0	11.2	18.0	25.1	29.2	32.1
Program Administration/ Net Cost Priv. Insurance	1.2	2.7	11.9	40.5	53.7	53.6	50.3	57.7
Public Health Activities	0.4	1.3	6.7	19.6	25.3	29.8	34.6	36.6
Research/Construction	1.7	5.3	11.6	24.5	29.0	30.8	34.8	35.3

Source: Health Care Financing Administration (2000). Office of the Actuary, National Health Statistics Group, *National Health Expenditures, Table 2.*
Research and development expenditures of drug companies, other manufacturers and providers of medical equipment and supplies are excluded from research expenditures, but are included in the expenditure class in which the product falls. The numbers may not add to totals because of rounding.

Table 15 Average Annual Percent Change of U.S. Health Expenditures

	1970	1980	1990	1993	1995	1997	1998
National Health Care	10.6	12.9	10.3	7.4	4.8	4.7	5.6
Health Services/Supplies	10.4	13.3	10.4	7.5	4.9	4.6	5.7
Personal Health Care	10.5	13.0	10.3	6.7	5.4	4.8	5.2
Hospital Care	11.7	13.9	8.8	5.8	3.3	3.0	3.4
Physician Services	9.9	12.8	11.8	5.7	4.6	4.5	5.4
Dental Services	9.1	11.1	7.8	6.8	6.1	7.6	5.3
Other Professional Services	8.8	16.3	15.8	9.6	8.1	7.0	8.3
Home Health Care	14.5	26.9	18.4	17.0	11.0	-2.2	-4.0
Drugs/Other Non-Durables	7.6	9.4	10.1	7.1	8.7	10.8	12.3
Prescriptive Drugs	7.5	8.2	12.2	8.7	10.6	14.0	15.4
Vision Products/Other Durables	9.6	8.8	9.2	3.4	6.1	6.7	2.7
Nursing Home Care	17.4	15.4	10.7	6.7	6.1	5.5	3.7
Other Personal Health Care	6.5	12.0	12.9	17.0	15.0	5.9	9.8
Program Administration/ Net Cost of Priv. Insurance	8.9	15.9	10.8	19.5	-2.8	-3.5	14.9
Public Health Activities	13.9	17.5	11.0	8.1	5.8	10.2	6.0
Research and Construction	12.2	8.1	8.4	5.3	1.0	8.8	1.6

Source: Health Care Financing Administration (2000). Office of the Actuary, National Health Statistics Group, National Health Expenditures, Table 2.
Research and development expenditures of drug companies and other manufacturers and providers of medical equipment and supplies are excluded from research expenditures, but are included in the expenditure class in which the product falls. The numbers may not add to totals because of rounding.

Table 16 Percent Distribution of U.S. Health Expenditures and Funding

Item	1960	1970	1980	1990	1993	1995	1997	1998
National Health Exp.	100,0	100,0	100,0	100,0	100,0	100,0	100,0	100,0
Private	75,2	62,2	57,6	59,5	57,1	54,1	53,8	54,5
Public	24,8	37,8	42,4	40,5	42,9	45,9	46,2	45,5
Federal	10,9	24,3	29,1	27,9	30,6	32,8	33,4	32,8
State and Local	13,9	13,5	13,3	12,6	12,2	13,1	12,8	12,7

Source: Health Care Financing Administration (2000). Office of the Actuary, National Health Statistics Group, National Health Expenditures..., Percent Distribution, Table 1.
The 1960 data comes from the previous release before November 1998.
The numbers may not add to totals because of rounding.

Table 17 Average Annual Percent Growth of U.S. Health Expenditures by Source of Funds

Item	1970	1980	1990	1993	1995	1997	1998
National Health Exp.	10,6	12,9	11,0	7,4	4,8	4,7	5,6
Private	8,5	12,1	11,3	6,1	2,4	4,8	6,9
Public	15,3	14,2	10,5	9,2	7,8	4,5	4,1
Federal	19,8	15,0	10,5	9,4	8,3	4,5	3,8
State and Local	10,2	12,7	10,4	8,6	6,6	4,6	4,7
U.S. population	1,2	0,9	1,0	1,0	0,9	0,9	0,9
GDP	7,0	10,4	6,6	5,0	4,6	5,9	4,9

Source: Health Care Financing Administration (2000). Office of the Actuary, National Health Statistics Group, National Health Expenditure, Average Annual Percent Growth from Previous Year Shown, Table 1. *The numbers may not add to totals. For 1960 were no corresponding data available*
Public is governmental health care funding e.g. in form of special programs for children etc. including the programs Medicare paid on the federal and Medicaid paid on the federal, state and local level. Private is every out-of-pocket-payment. Private insurance expenditures are classified as third-party-payments because of their indirect payment character.

Table 18 Aggregate Amounts of Personal Health Care Expenditures by Source of Funds (in U.S. $)

Year	Total	Out-of Pock. Paym.	Third-Party Payments								
			Total	Priv. Health Insurance	Other Priv. Funds	Government					
						Total	Fed.	State and Local	Medicare *	Medicaid **
1960	23,6	13,1	10,6	5,0	0,4	5,1	2,1	3,0	--	--
1970	63,8	24,9	38,9	14,8	1,6	22,5	14,7	7,8	7,3	5,1
1980	217,0	60,3	156,8	62,0	7,8	87,0	63,4	23,6	36,4	24,8
1990	614,7	145,0	469,6	207,7	20,8	241,1	177,0	64,2	108,6	71,4
1993	790,5	167,1	623,5	265,2	26,8	331,4	252,3	79,1	144,7	115,8
1995	879,1	170,5	708,6	286,3	31,1	391,2	299,0	92,2	180,8	137,2
1997	968,6	189,1	779,6	312,4	36,3	430,9	333,4	97,5	205,6	152,2
1998	1019,3	199,5	819,8	337,0	37,9	444,9	343,6	101,3	210,5	159,6

Source: Health Care Financing Administration (2000). Office of the Actuary, National Health Statistics Group, *National Health Expenditures, Table 4. Numbers may not add to totals because of rounding.*

*Subset of Federal Funds
** Subset of Federal and State and Local Funds

Table 19 Percent Distribution of U.S. Health Expenditures by Source of Funds (Total is 100 percent)

Year	Third-Party Payments						Medicare *	Medicaid **
	Total	Private Health Insurance	Other Private Funds	Government				
				Total	Federal	State and Local		
1960	44,7	21,2	1,8	21,7	9,0	12,6	--	--
1970	61,0	23,2	2,6	35,3	23,0	12,2	11,4	7,9
1980	72,2	28,6	3,6	40,1	29,2	10,9	16,8	11,4
1990	76,4	33,8	3,4	39,2	28,8	10,4	17,7	11,6
1993	78,9	33,6	3,4	41,9	31,9	10,0	18,3	14,6
1995	80,6	32,6	3,5	44,5	34,0	10,5	20,6	15,6
1997	80,5	32,3	3,7	44,5	34,4	10,1	21,2	15,7
1998	80,4	33,1	3,7	43,6	33,7	9,9	20,6	15,7

Source: Health Care Financing Administration (2000). Office of the Actuary, National Health Statistics Group, *National Health Expenditures, Table 4.* Numbers may not add to totals because of rounding.

*Subset of Federal Funds
** Subset of Federal and State and Local Funds

Table 20 Payment Plans and Effects on Prices and Care Delivery

Plan	Inputed exp. per person *	Admission rate per 100 Persons	Hospital days per 100 Persons	Face-to-Face Visits	Preventive Visits (Correlation efficient r)
HMO experi-mental	439	8,4	49	4,3	0,55
HMO control	469	8,3	38	4,7	0,60
Fee-For-Service (FFS)					
Free	609	13,8	83	4,2	0,41
25% co-payment FFS	620	10,0	87	3,5	0,32
95% co-payment FFS	459	10,5	46	2,9	0,29

Source: Manning, Williard G. et al (June 7th 1984). *A controlled Trial of the effect of a Pre-paid Group Practice on Use of Services, Tables 1 and 2.*
*In 1983 US $. The listing includes out-of-plan use for HMO enrollees

Table 21 Medical Care Markets and Economical Interrelations

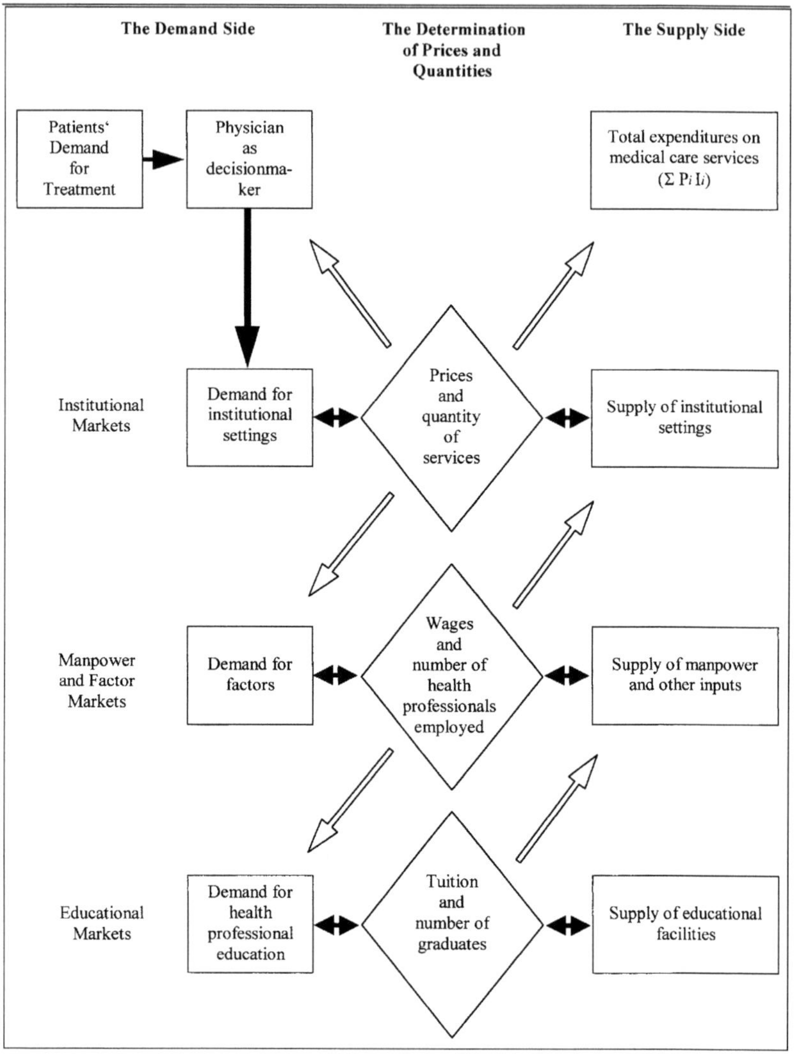

Source: Koengstvedt, Peter R. (1996). *The Managed Health Care Handbook.* Figure 3-1. Page 38.

Table 22 Map of Eastern North America

Source: *Diercke Weltatlas (World Atlas)* (1985/1986). Page 149. The border line between Eastern and Western Germany (See 'Zum Vergleich') was removed from the original.

Table 23 Map of Michigan

Source: Hildebrand's Travel Atlas (1998/1999). *United States and Canada*. Page 63.

Table 24 Map of the City of Marquette

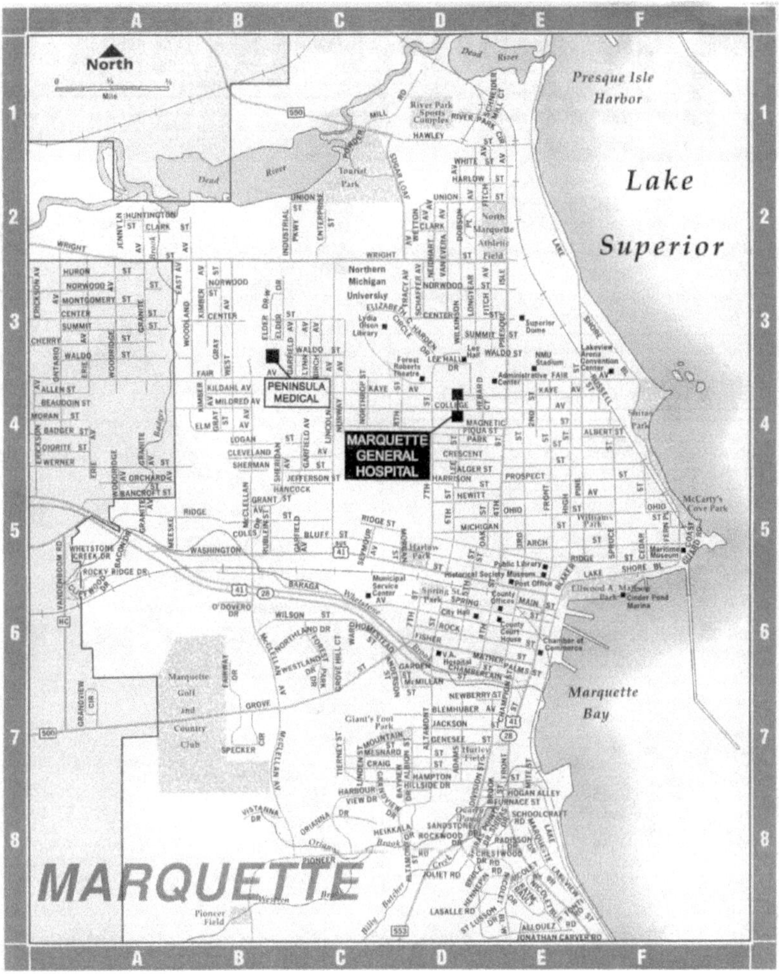

Source: MGHS Community Relations Department. Patient Information. Based on *Information Pages* (1996). Ameritech Publishing Inc.

Table 25 Logo and Picture of MGHS

MARQUETTE
GENERAL HEALTH SYSTEM

Source: Marquette General Health System (1999). Pictures

Table 26 Upper Peninsula Health Care Network (UPHCN)

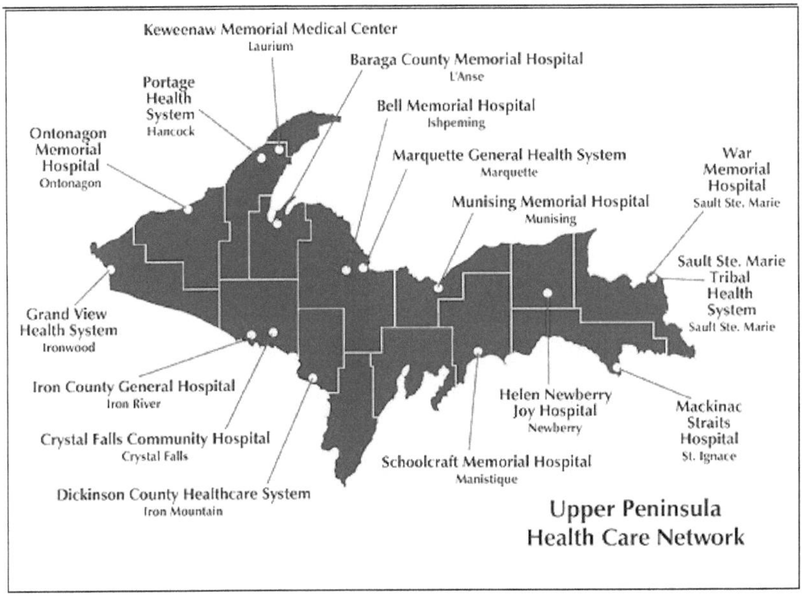

Source: Upper Peninsula Health Care Network (1999). Services – Overview. Electronic source available: [http://www.uphcn.org/uphcn/service.html 03/10/99 16:44:11].

Table 27 Provider Network MGH

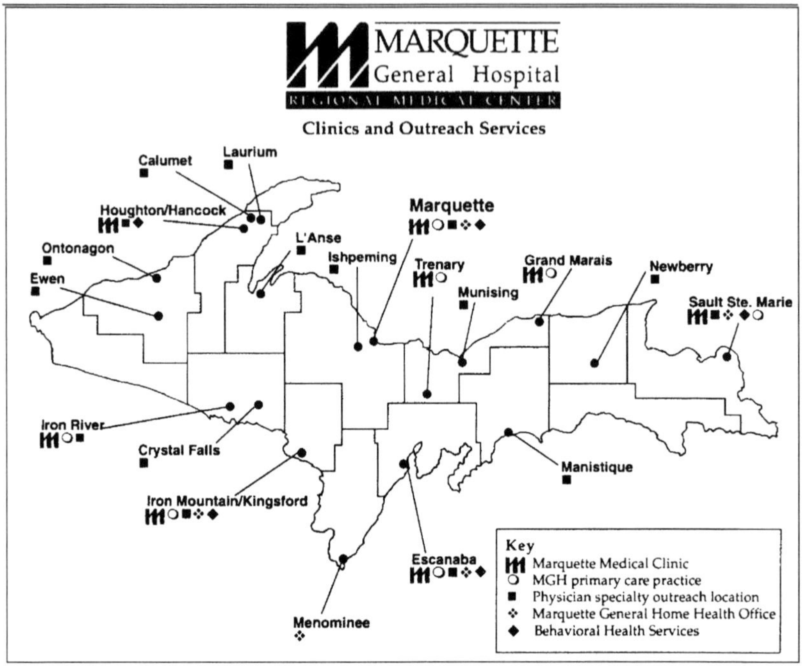

Source: Marquette General Hospital, Community Relations and Marketing Department (March 1996). *Friends & Neighbors Caring for You, the Services of Marquette General Hospital.* Marquette, MI.

Table 28 Organizational Chart of MGH(S)

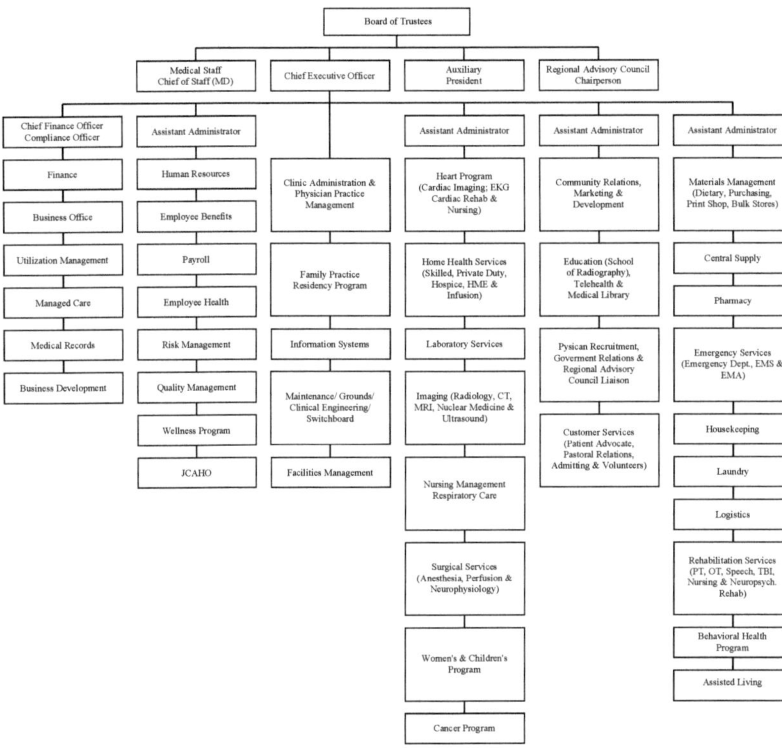

Source: Marquette General Hospital, W. R. Nemacheck (CEO) (February 16th 1999). *Organizational Chart*. Marquette MI.

Table 29 Business Ethics of MGH(S)

Marquette General Hospital

Mission, Vision and Values

Mission

Our *Mission* is to provide access to primary and tertiary health care services
to improve the health status of the residents
of Marquette County, the Upper Peninsula and the surrounding region.

Vision

Our *Vision* is to provide quality care,
cost effective patient care services
developed with excellence in patient care and customer service
which allow us to prosper as a business
and invest in the health and well-being of the residents of the Region,
partnering and collaborating with others whose goals align with ours.

Values

In order to accomplish our mission, we must strive to meet our *Values* of:

Competency

People are our most important asset and are the source of our strength. Having the right people doing the right things at the right time is essential to our reputation and vitality.

Customer Service

Excellence in patient care is the focus of everything we do. Our work must be done with our customers in mind, providing better service than our competitors and exceeding the expectations of every customer.

Quality

:Continuous quality improvement is essential to our service. We must strive for excellence in everything we do. To achieve customer satisfaction, the quality of our services must be a number one priority.

Safety

Safety of our customers, staff, visitors and others cannot be compromised and is built into everything we do.

Stewardship

Our responsibility is to prudently manage and utilize our resources to improve the health status of the communities we serve.

Teamwork

Employees, Medical Staff, Board and external partners comprise our Team and are essential to the success in meeting our mission. We must treat each other with trust and respect.

Source: Marquette General Hospital. Mission, Vision and Values (1998). Marquette, MI.

Table 30 MGHS Strategic Development Questionnaire

This is the list of questions that were sent out as questionnaire to all Department Heads and Program Directors at MGHS.

How do you rate the following issues?

1.) Have employees found MGHS a satisfying place to work at?

very much ☐ much ☐ don't know ☐ not much ☐ not at all ☐

2.) Do you think MGHS employees are proud to work for the largest health care provider in the Upper Peninsula of Michigan?

very much ☐ much ☐ don't know ☐ not much ☐ not at all ☐

3.) Do you agree that strategic thinking is one of the most important issues besides other management tasks to ensure MGHS's future financial success?

very much ☐ much ☐ don't know ☐ not much ☐ not at all ☐

4.) Do you think health care by MGHS meets the demands of the customer more efficiently if it integrates a broader range of services and experiences?

very much ☐ much ☐ don't know ☐ not much ☐ not at all ☐

5.) Do you think adding services like health insurance offerings makes MGHS less dependent on government based payment plans like Medicare and Medicaid?

very much ☐ much ☐ don't know ☐ not much ☐ not at all ☐

6.) Do you think that broadening of services offered by MGHS lead to a lowering of their respective quality?

very much ☐ much ☐ don't know ☐ not much ☐ not at all ☐

7.) Do you think customers are attracted more by renovated and new facilities than by any internal show-pieces like excellent services?

very much ☐ much ☐ don't know ☐ not much ☐ not at all ☐

8.) Do you agree that modernizing facilities technically enable the medical, nursing and administrative staff to perform their work more efficiently?

very much ☐ much ☐ don't know ☐ not much ☐ not at all ☐

9.) Do you think a shiny and well-equipped work-environment affects the employee's motivation to work?

very much ☐ much ☐ don't know ☐ not much ☐ not at all ☐

10.) Do you think friendly and open-minded doctors and nurses make patients feel safe and make them come back if they have further or new health problems?

very much ☐ much ☐ don't know ☐ not much ☐ not at all ☐

11.) Do you assume that more offerings in special medical research and treatment prevents patients seeking health care at competing health care institutions?

very much ☐ much ☐ don't know ☐ not much ☐ not at all ☐

12.) How do you rate the importance of in-house training for employees to keep abreast of new management strategies, new ways of medical treatment or nursing behavior etc.?

very much ☐ much ☐ don't know ☐ not much ☐ not at all ☐

13.) Even if it is costly do think head-hunting for well-known physicians pays off in attracting customers?

very much ☐ much ☐ don't know ☐ not much ☐ not at all ☐

14.) Would you say that without active recruiting of specialists, no competent physician etc. would voluntary seek employment in the rural Upper Peninsula?

very much ☐ much ☐ don't know ☐ not much ☐ not at all ☐

15.) How do you rate the recruitment of top-ranking physicians as a show-piece beneficial to MGHS?

very much ☐ much ☐ don't know ☐ not much ☐ not at all ☐

16.) Do you think provider alliances of non-profit hospitals like the 'UP Health Care Network' strengthen the position at negotiations with payment contractors like Medicare?

very much ☐ much ☐ don't know ☐ not much ☐ not at all ☐

17.) Do you think networking with other regional competitors in providing services or sharing information keeps patients from seeking health care outside the Upper Peninsula?

very much ☐ much ☐ don't know ☐ not much ☐ not at all ☐

18.) Do you think networking with competitors hurt the economical position of MGHS?

very much ☐ much ☐ don't know ☐ not much ☐ not at all ☐

19.) Would you agree that lobbying with politicians pays off in healthcare legislation beneficial to hospitals like MGHS?

very much ☐ much ☐ don't know ☐ not much ☐ not at all ☐

20.) Do you think that advertising a positive image by publications or sponsoring non-medical community events fosters MGHS's profit margin positively?

very much ☐ much ☐ don't know ☐ not much ☐ not at all ☐

21.) Would you say individual health and religion are interrelated areas?

very much ☐ much ☐ don't know ☐ not much ☐ not at all ☐

22.) Do you feel knowledgeable enough, what to answer when subordinates or customers ask about MGHS's management strategy?

very much ☐ much ☐ don't know ☐ not much ☐ not at all ☐

23.) Do you think managers at MGHS know, if subordinates are satisfied with their job or not?

very much ☐ much ☐ don't know ☐ not much ☐ not at all ☐

24.) Would you say that using informal relationships with the upper level management is the best way to keep informed about plans of the upper management?

very much ☐ much ☐ don't know ☐ not much ☐ not at all ☐

25.) How do you rate the importance of monetary incentives versus non-monetary incentives like 'Employee of the Month' for the employee's performance?

very much ☐ much ☐ don't know ☐ not much ☐ not at all ☐

26.) Do you think the implementation of 'Result Share' makes employees more aware of MGHS's overall business besides individual job description and compensation?

very much ☐ much ☐ don't know ☐ not much ☐ not at all ☐

27.) Do you think that tying employees to MGHS's economical success by 'Result Share' makes the failure of future unionization campaigns more likely?

very much ☐ much ☐ don't know ☐ not much ☐ not at all ☐

Source: Neunert, T. (1999). MGHS Strategic Development Questionnaire.

Contact

Marquette General Health System Inc.
580 West College Avenue
Marquette, Michigan 49855
USA
Homepage: www.mgh.org

Universität Hannover (University of Hanover)
Welfengarten 1
30167 Hannover
Germany
Homepage: www.uni-hannover.de

Thomas Neunert
Isernhagener Strasse 18
30161 Hannover
Germany

Phone (from the U.S.): (011-) 49-511-388 41 24
Cell Phone (from the U.S.): (011-) 49-171-950 31 18
Email: Thomas.Neunert@t-online.de

References

Allen, R. W. (1976). *Hospital Planning Handbook.*
New York NY: John Wiley and Sons Inc. Page 1.

American Hospital Association (February 1999). *Health Care's 100 Most Wired.* In: Hospitals and Health Networks.

American Public Health Organization (1999). *Balanced Budget Act of 1997 Fact Sheet.* Electronic source available:
http://www.apha.org/legislative/factsheets/balbudget_fs.htm [3/4/99 10:22 AM].

American Hospital Association and American Association of Medical Colleges (April 1 1999). *Letter to Affiliates.* Chicago IL. AHA. Page 2.

Bacon, D. C. (April 1989). *Nonprofits Groups: An Unfair Edge?* In: Nation's Business Magazine. U.S. Chamber of Commerce. Washington DC. Page 33-34.

Benham, L. and A. (October 1972). *Regulating through the Professions: ...* In: Journal of Law and Economics.
New York NY: Oxford University Press. Page 15.

Bertalanffy, von (1972). In: Dorsch, Friedrich (1994). *Psychologisches Woerterbuch (Psychological Dictionary),* 12th edition.
Goettingen, Germany: Verlag Hans Huber. Page 782.

Blanke, Bernhard (1994). *Governance im Gesundheitswesen (Governance in the Health System).* In: Krankheit und Gemeinwohl (Disease and Public Weal). Opladen: Leske und Budrich, Germany. Page 15.

Collins, S. (November 29th 1993). *A Bitter Financial Pill.* In: U.S. News and World Report. Washington DC: U.S. News Inc. Page 83-96.

Costillo, L. B. (October 13th 1985). *Anti-Trust Enforcement in Health Care: ...* In: New England Journal of Medicine, 313 (14).
Boston MA: Massachusetts Medical Society.

Desai, K. R. et al. (September 1998). *Hospital Conversions from For-Profit to Non-Profit Status: The Other Side of the Story*. In: Medical Care Research and Review, Vol.55 no.3. Thousand Oaks CA: Sage Publications Inc.

Development Dimensions International, Personal Development Folder including: *Key Principles [and] Self-evaluation/Core Skills for Building Commitment/Facilitating Improved Performance/Following Up to Support Improvement*. MCMXCVI: Pittsburgh PA: DDI Inc.

Downs, Gabriel N. and Michael C. (1999). *Marquette, Images of America.* Charleston, SC: Arcadia Publishing Inc.

Drucker, P. F. (July/August 1989). *What Business Can Learn from Nonprofits.* In: Harvard Business Review. Boston MA: HBS Publishing Inc. Page 89.

Havighurst, C. C. (Winter 1980). *Anti-Trust Enforcement in the Medical Services Industry*. In: Milbank Memorial Fund Quarterly, 58 (1).
New York NY: Milbank Memorial Fund.

Havighurst, C. C. (editor) (1974). *Regulating Health Facilities Construction.* Washington, D.C.: American Enterprise Institute for Public Policy Research.

Health Care Financing Administration (1999). *Index of the National Health Expenditures Aggregate*, *Table 09*. Electronic source available:
http://www.hcfa.gov./stats/nhe~oact/tables/t09.htm [12/10/99 5:13 PM].

Health Care Financing Administration (2000). *National Health Expenditures, Table 2*. Electronic source available:
http://www.hcfa.gov/stats/nhe~oact/tables/t2.htm [02/12/00 2:12 PM].

Health Care Financing Administration (2000). *National Health Expenditures , Table 4*. Electronic source available:
http://www.hcfa.gov/stats/nhe~oact/tables/t4.htm [02/12/00 2:00 PM].

Health Care Financing Administration (2000). *National Health Expenditures Projections, Table 1*. Electronic source available:
http://www.hcfa.gov/stats/NHE-Proj/proj1998/tables/table1.htm
[02/12/00 3:09 PM].

Health Care Management Review (1991).
Gaithersburg MD: Aspen Publishers Inc.

Hunger, D. J. and Wheelen, T. L. (1998). *Strategic Management and Business Policy: Entering the 21st Century*, 6th edition.
Reading MA, Menlo Park CA, New York NY: Addison Wesley Longman Inc.

Johnson, S. (President of the Michigan Health and Hospital Association) (1999). *Key Messages – 1999 Day at the Capitol*. Lansing MI.

Interviews (*MGHS-SMAUSHC1-9* and *MGHS-SMAUSHC-CEO,-CFO,-BOT*) including statements of the Chief Executive Officer, Assistant Administrators, Department Heads, Board of Trustees and others affiliated with MGHS (December 1999 and January 2000). Key to the anonymous interview data is stored at the author of this thesis (Thomas Neunert).

Joint Commission in Accreditation of Healthcare Organizations (1999). *Home Page*. Electronic source available: http://www.jcaho.org/mainmenu.html [8/3/99 11:32 AM].

Kierkegaard, S. in: Calvin, W. H. (1996). *How Brains Think – Evolving Intelligence, Then and Now.*
New York NY: Basic Books/Hooper Collins Publishers Inc.

Koengstvedt, P. R. (1996). *The Managed Health Care Handbook*, 3rd edition. Gaithersburg MD: Aspen Publishers, Inc.

Lancaster, J. (Editor) (1999). *Nursing Issues in Leading and Managing Change*, St. Louis MO: Mosby Inc. Page 7-9.

Learner, A. N. (Summer 1984). *Federal Trade Commission: Anti-Trust Activities in the Health Care Services Field*, Anti-Trust Bulletin, 29 (2). Page 205-224.

Leibenluft, R. F. and Pollard, M. R. (May 1981). *Anti-Trust Scrutiny of the Health Professions: ...*, Vanderbilt Law Review34 (4).
Nashville TN: Vanderbilt University Law School.

Leichter, H. M. (1997). *Health Care Policy Reform in America: Innovations from the States*, 2nd edition. Armonk NY: M.E. Sharpe. Page 19-21.

Leeds, H. S. (1996). *Certificate of Need: Up for Revision.*
In: Health System Review Vol. 29.

Litman, T. J. and Robins, L. S. (1997). *Health Politics and Policy*, 3rd edition, Delmar Publishers, Albany, NY. Page 445.

Long, D. E. and Golden, J.(1989). *The American General Hospital.*
New York NY: Cornell University Press. Page 4.

Luke R. D., Begun J. W. and Pointer D. D. (January 1989). *Quasi-Firms: Strategic Inter-organizational Forms in the Health Care Industry.*
Academy of Management Review.
Briarcliff Manor NY: Academy of Management. Page 9-19.

Manning, Williard G. et al. (June 7th 1984). *A Controlled Trial of the Effect of a Prepaid Group Practice on Use of Services, Tables 1 and 2.*
New England Journal of Medicine , 310 (23).
Boston MA: Massachusetts Medical Society.

March, J.G. and Simon, H.A. (1958). *Organizations.*
New York NY: John Wiley and Sons Inc..

Marquette County (2000). Information site. Electronic source available: http://medc.michigan.org/stats/profiles/52.htm [2000, May 20, 12:58]

Marquette General Hospital (1998). *Mission, Vision and Values.* Marquette, MI.

Marquette General Hospital, Community Relations and Marketing Department (March 1996). *Friends & Neighbors Caring for You, the Services of Marquette General Hospital.* Marquette, MI.

Marquette General Hospital. Community Relations and Marketing Department (February 1996). *Hotline*, Volume 2, Issue 2. Marquette, MI.

Marquette General Hospital (2000). Fiscal Year 1999, Finance Information of the CFO, January 2000. Marquette MI.

Marquette General Hospital (September 1996). Information Folder (including employee and institutional information). Marquette MI.

Marquette General Hospital (March 1999). Information Folder (including employee and institutional information), Marquette MI.

Marquette General Hospital, W. R. Nemacheck (CEO) (February 16th 1999). *Organizational Chart*. Marquette MI.

Marquette General Health System (1999). *Letter of Intent, Critical Access Hospital Agreement* (Draft). Marquette MI.

Marquette General Health System (1999). Pictures.

Matousek and Associates (1995), *1995 Awareness Study MGH – Findings*. Green Bay WI.

Melnick, Glenn A. and Feinstein, Paul J. (Winter 1984). *Congressional Voting Behavior on Hospital Legislation: An Exploratory Study*.
Journal of Health Politics, Policy and Law.
Durham NC: Duke University Press.

Michigan Department of Career Development/Employment Agency (2000). Labor Market Data. Electronic source available:
http://www.michlmi.org/lmadata/laus/lausdocs/103lf96.htm and
http://www.michlmi.org /lausdocs/103lf00.htm [5/20/00 14:10].

Michigan Department of Career Development/Employment Agency/Labor Market Analysis Section (2000). Labor Market Data. Electronic source available:
http://www.michlmi.org/lmadata/allareas/alldocs/all9601.htm and
http://www.michlmi.org/lmadata/allareas/alldocs /all0001.htm [5/20/00 13:06].

Michigan Health and Hospital Association (February/March 1999) *Health PAC News*. Lansing MI.

Michigan Health and Hospital Association (1998). *Hospital Community Benefits Survey*. Lansing MI.

Michigan Health and Hospital Association (1999). *No Margin, No Mission – The Financial Realities of Michigan's Nonprofit Hospitals*. Lansing MI. Page 3.

Michigan Information Center/Department of Management and Budget (April 30th 1999). *Michigan Trivia*, April 30 1999. Electronic source available: http://www.state.mi.us/dmb/mic/news/trivia.htm [5/20/00 12:52].

Moody's State Health Care Review (August 1995). *Michigan, Marquette General Hospital*. Analysts: K. M. Sitterman, B. E. Gordon. New York NY.

MWM Marketing Research and Consulting (1999). *1999 Awareness Study MGH: Hospital Service Area Awareness and Attitudes - Topline Findings*. Arlington Heights IL, 1999. Page 2.

Neunert, T. (1999). *MGHS Strategic Development Questionnaire*.

Nielsen, R. P. (Summer 1982) *SMR Forum: Strategic Piggybacking – A Self-subsidizing Strategy for Nonprofit Institutions*. In: Sloan Management Review. Cambridge MA: Sloan Management Review Association. Page 65-69.

Office of Rural Health Policy (February 1999). *Rural Hospitals, Clinics, and Networks; Rural Hospital Flexibility Program; Rural Health Outreach and Rural Network Grant Program*
In: About the Office of Rural Health Policy. Electronic source available: http://www.nal.usda.gov/orhp/orhpstmt.htm [04/01/99 14:27:43].

Patel, Kant and Rushefsky, Mark E. (1995). *Health Care Politics and Policy in America*. M.E. Sharpe Inc., Armonk NY. Page 15-16, 36 and 51 pp.

PictureTel (1996). *Case Study: Training and Education* [at MGH].

In: Healthcare Solutions from PictureTel Inc./Industry Overview. Andover MA.

Provan, K.G. (July 1984). *Interorganizational Cooperation and Decision-Making Autonomy in a Consortium Multihospital System.*
In: Academy of Management Review.
Briarcliff Manor NY: Academy of Management. Page 494-504.

Puskin, D. S. (Office for the Advancement of Telehealth) (Spring 1999). *From the Feds ... OAT: Giving High Tech Ideas the Human Touch.*
In: Rural Health News. Portland ME. University of Southern Maine.

Raffel, M. W. (1980). *The U.S. Health System – Origins and Functions.*
New York NY: John Wiley and Sons Inc. Page 2-7.

Schermerhorn, J. R. Jr. (1996). *Management and Organizational Behavior – Essentials.* New York NY: John Wiley and Sons Inc.

Schmidt, Manfred G. (1995). *Woerterbuch zur Politik (Political Dictionary).*
Alfred Kroener Verlag, Stuttgart, Germany. Page 428.

Simon, J. G. (1987). *The treatment of nonprofit Organizations: A Review of Federal and State Policies in: The Nonprofit Sector: A Research Handbook.* Edited by Powell, W. W. New Haven: Yale University Press. Page 67-98.

Skloot, E. (January/February 1983). *Should Not-for-profits Go into Business?*
In: Harvard Business Review. Boston MA: HBS Publishing. Page 21.

The Rural Work group of the Interagency Task Force on Children's Health Insurance Outreach (1999). *Why is rural important?* Electronic source available: http://www.nal.usda.gov/orhp/chip2.htm [04/01/99 14:14:53].

Travel & Recreation Association (1999). *Michigan's Upper Peninsula.* Iron Mountain MI.

Tribrook Inc. (January 1996). *Strategic Plan 1996 Marquette General Hospital.*

Upper Peninsula Health Care Network (1999). *Services – Overview.* Electronic source available: http://www.uphcn.org/uphcn/service.html [03/10/99 16:44:11].

Upper Peninsula Health Plan (1999). *Home Page.* Electronic source available: http://www.uphp.com [03/10/99 16:47:30].

U.S. Congress (1997). *Balanced Budget Act of 1997.* In: Federal Register. Electronic source available: http://www.access.gpo.gov/index.html [3/4/99 10:28 AM].

U.S. Representative Nussle (March 16th 1999). Discussion Draft, *A Bill to Promote and Improve Access to Health Services in Rural Areas.* U.S. Congress. U.S. House of Representatives. Washington DC.

Webb, C. (May 3rd 1999). *Analyst: Bottom-line Thinking Hurts Hospitals' Most Marketable Assets.* In: AHA News, Vol. 35, No. 17. American Hospital Association. Chicago IL.

Webb, C. (May 3rd 1999). *Win Back Alienated Patients or Face Consequences, Hospital Leaders Told.* In: AHA News Vol. 35, No. 17. American Hospital Association. Chicago IL.

Weinert, A. B. (1998). Organisationspsychologie (Organizational Psychology), 4th edition. Weinheim: Beltz/Psychologie Verlags Union. Page 54.

Wilson, F. A. and Neuhauser, D. (1982). *Health Services in the United States.* Boston MA: Ballinger Publishing Company. Page 120.

Further Readings and Informational Sources

Altman, S. H. and Reinhardt, U. E. (May 1996). *Strategic Choices for a Changing Health Care System*, Baxter Health Policy Review, Series No. 2.
Chicago IL: Health Administration Press.

Blanke, B. and Bandemer, S. von (editors) (November 2000). *Handbuch zur Verwaltungsreform (Handbook regarding the Reform of the Administrative Sector),* 2nd edition. Leverkusen, Germany: Leske und Budrich.

Bowman, J. S. (1991). *Ethical Frontiers in Public Management, Seeking New Strategies for Resolving Ethical Dilemmas.*
San Francisco CA: Jossey-Bass Inc.

Burell, G. (1993). *Sociological Paradigms and Organizational Analysis.*
Aldershot, United Kingdom: Arena Inc.

Callahan, D. (April 1998). *False Hopes: Why America's Quest for Perfect Health is a Prescription for Disaster.*
New York NY: Simon and Schuster Inc.

Callahan, D. (May 1999). *False Hopes: Overcoming the Obstacles to a Sustainable, Affordable Medicine.* Piscataway NJ: Rutgers University Press.

Carnahan, G. R. (July/August 1999). *Selecting a Strategy – Internal and External Considerations, Seminar text/outline in 'MGT 436 - Strategic Management'*, 2nd Summer Session. Northern Michigan University, Marquette MI.

Cochran, C. L. and Malone E. F. (1999). *Public Policy, Perspectives and Choices*, 2nd edition. New York NY: The McGraw-Hill Companies Inc.

Costin, H. (1994). *Reading in Total Quality Management*, Harcourt Brace College Publishers, New York NY, Page 143.

Disney Institute (1999). *Professional Development Programs: The Disney Approach/Programs for the Healthcare Industry*. Electronic source available: http://www.disney.com/DisneyWorld/ProfessionalPrograms/index.html [03/25/99 01:51:44 AM].

Feldstein, P. J. (1993). *Health Care Economics*, 4th edition. Albany NY: Delmar Publishers Inc.

Feldstein, P. J. (August 1999). *Health Policy Issues: An Economic Perspective*, 2nd edition. Chicago IL: Health Administration Press.

Herzlinger, R. (1997). *Market Driven Health Care – Who Wins, Who Loses in the Transformation of America's Largest Service Industry*. Reading MA: Perseus Books Inc.

Kuczewski, M. G. (1999). *An Ethic Casebook for Hospitals*. Washington DC: Georgetown University Press.

Lee, T. W. (1999). *Using Qualitative Methods in Organizational Research*. Thousand Oaks, CA: Sage Publications Inc.

Maine Rural Health Research Center, Edmund S. Muskie School of Public Service (1999). *Tracking Changes in Rural Health Care*. In: Rural Health News Vol. 5, No. 3. Portland ME: University of Southern Maine.

Manheim, J. B. and Rich, R. C. (1991) *Empirical Political Analysis: Research Methods in Political Science*, 3rd edition.
White Plains NY: Longman Publishing Group.

Marquette General Hospital and Upper Peninsula Medical Center (Spring 1999). *Excellence in Education*. Marquette MI.

Michigan Department of Community Health (March 13th 1998). Certificate of Need Program, *Annual Activity Report October 1996 - September 1997*. Lansing MI.

Office of Management and Budget (OMB) (December 21, 1998), *Alternative Approaches to Defining Metropolitan and Non-metropolitan Areas*.
In: Federal Register Vol. 63, No. 244.

O'Sullivan, E. and Rassel, G. (1995). *Research Methods for Public Administrators*. White Plains NY: Longman Publishing Group.

Osborne, D. and Gaebler, T. (1992). Reinventing Government: *How the Entrepreneurial Spirit is Transforming the Public Sector*.
Reading MA: Addison-Wesley Inc.

Pfeffer, J. (1997). *New Directions for Organizational Theory: Problems and Prospects*. New York NY: Oxford University Press.

Reid, J. (1996). *A Telemedicine Primer: Understanding the Issues, Innovative Medical Innovations.*

Robertson. T. S. and Kassarjian H. H. (1991). *Handbook of Consumer Behavior*. Eaglewood Cliffs NJ: Prentice Hall.

Rosen, L. S., Michigan Hospital Association/Service Corporation/Data Services (1999) *Facts about Michigan's Population and Health Care Industry.* Lansing MI.

Schliewert, Günter (1997). *USA – Handbuch für Auswanderer (USA – Handbook for Immigrants)*, 2nd edition. Stuttgart, Germany: Pietsch Verlag.

Simon, Michael (2000). *Krankenhauspolitik in der Bundesrepublik Deutschland (Hospital Policy in the Federal Republic of Germany).* Wiesbaden, Germany: Westdeutscher Verlag.

Social Security Administration (SSA) (1995). *A Brief History of Social Security – Social Security 60th Anniversary*, SSA Publication No. 21-059, ICN 44 00 00.

Social Security Administration (SSA) (October 1998). *The Future of Social Security*. SSA Publication No. 05-10055, ICN 46 25 60.

Stevens, R. (February 1999). *In Sickness and in Wealth: American Hospitals in the Twentieth Century*. Baltimore MD: John Hopkins University Press.

Stewart, C. T. Jr. (1995). *Healthy, Wealthy or Wise – Issues in American Health Care Policy.* Armonk NY: M.E. Sharpe Inc.

Telehealth Magazine (June 1999) *Beyond Feasibility: Neonatal Teleradiology Shows Cost Benefits,* Vol. 5, No. 3. San Francisco CA: Miller Freeman.

The Commonwealth Fund (Diverse documents and research results on health and social issues). Electronic source available: http://www.cmwf.org [11/5/99 04:12 PM].

The Rural Information Center Health Service (RICHS) (1999). *Federal Support for Rural Health – A Compendium of Federal Programs Programs that Support the Provision of Health Care in Rural Areas*. Electronic source available: http://www.nal.usda.gov/ric/richspub/rural_pg.htm [04/01/99 2:22:27 AM].

Theisen, M. R. (1998). *Wissenschaftliches Arbeiten (Scientific Work)*, 9th edition. Muenchen (Munich), Germany: Verlag Franz Vahlen.

Tiber Group Inc. (1999). *New Rules, New Roles for Rural Health Care Providers – Snapshots for the Future*, Chicago IL.

Trotter, J. P. (1995). *The Quest for Cost-Effectiveness in Healthcare: Achieving Clinical Excellence While Controlling Costs*.
American Hospital Association (AHA)/American Hospital Publishing Inc.

U.S. Department of Labor, Pension and Welfare Administration (1999). *Questions and Answers: Recent Changes in Health Care Law*, Washington D.C.
Electronic source available:
http://www.purl.access.gpo.gov/GPO/LPS2902 [12/12/99 10:43 AM].

U. S. General Accounting Office (GAO) (February 1999), Report to Congressional Requesters, *Physician Shortage Areas: Medicare Incentive Payments not an Effective Approach to Improve Access.*
Publication-No. GAO/HEHS-99-36.

U.S. Congress (104th/second session), House of Representatives, Committee on Commerce, Subcommittee on Health and the Environment (March 7th 1996). *Health Care Reform: Reforming the Small Business Market Place and the Individual Health Insurance Market*.

Videoconferencing Insight (1999). *No. 99/04 - 99/06.*
Hove, United Kingdom: IMP Publishers Inc.

Williamson, O. E. (January 1993). *The Nature of the Firm: Origins, Evolution, and Development*. New York NY: Oxford University Press.

Wolper, L. I. (1995). *Health Care Administration*, 2nd edition.
Gaithersburg MD: Aspen Publishers Inc.

Yin, Robert K. (1994). *Case Study Research – Design and Methods*, 2nd edition,
Applied Social Science Research Methods Series, Volume 5.
Thousand Oaks CA: Sage Publications Inc.